The
Investor's Guide to
Traded Options

The
Investor's Guide to
Traded Options

DAVID FORD

FINANCIAL TIMES

PITMAN PUBLISHING

PITMAN PUBLISHING
128 Long Acre, London WC2E 9AN

A Division of Longman Group UK Limited

First published in Great Britain 1994

British Library Cataloguing in Publication Data
A CIP catalogue record for this book can be obtained from the British Library.

ISBN 0 273 60704 9

Typeset by PanTek Arts Ltd, Maidstone, Kent.
Printed and bound in Great Britain by Biddles, Guildford and King's Lynn

It is the Publishers' policy to use paper produced from sustainable forests.

CONTENTS

Preface   vii

PART ONE – THE FOUNDATIONS   I

 1 **Introduction**   3

 2 **Basic Concept and Terminology**   9

 3 **Basic Trades**   19

 4 **Index Options**   31

PART TWO – TRADING   37

 5 **Pricing Traded Options**   39

 6 **Strategies: Buying Calls**   53

 7 **Strategies: Writing (Selling) Calls**   59

 8 **Strategies: Buying Puts**   67

 9 **Strategies: Writing (Selling) Puts**   71

10 **Advanced Strategies**   73

11 **Risk Management**   95

12 **Trading and Settlement**   105

13 **Choosing a Broker**   113

14 **Choosing a Stock**   119

PART THREE – ADDITIONAL INFORMATION   135

15 Other Derivative Instruments   137

16 The London Clearing House and Margin   149

17 Corporate Events   155

18 Options in Portfolio Management   161

19 Regulation   167

20 Advanced Options Pricing Theories   173

Appendix A   Answers   185
Appendix B   Contract specifications   191
Appendix C   Option stockbrokers for private investors   193
Appendix D   LIFFE index and equity options and their
*   expiry cycles*   199
Appendix E   Further questions and answers   201
Glossary   207
Index   213

PREFACE

I was persuaded to write this book after a number of years in traded options, lecturing to both market professionals and private investors. For market professionals there are a number of excellent books available, although all are at an advanced level, but for the private investor there are, to date, just two books covering the introduction of traded options. I have therefore aimed the book specifically at private investors in the hope that it will dispel many of the myths and misconceptions surrounding traded options and encourage private investors to use options.

As the book will demonstrate, traded options can be most things to most people, allowing the management of risk in a way no other investment vehicle can. Their flexibility allows traded options to increase risk and thus obtain very high returns or alternatively to decrease risk and insure an individual shareholding or a portfolio against an adverse price movement.

The advantages of traded options over other investments include a limited outlay to control large amounts of stock, limited risk when buying options and, the ability to make a profit in a falling, rising or neutral market.

The book is divided into three parts. Part One – The Foundations, covers Chapters 1 to 4 and looks at the basic concept of traded options – what is an option, what is the terminology associated with them, how and why they work and the foundations for successful future trading.

Part Two – Trading, covers the pricing of options (Chapter 5), the different component parts and the effect they have on an options price. The four basic trades associated with options are covered in depth in Chapters 6–9 looking at what to trade, when and why. Chapter 10 looks at combining two or more of the four basic trades to alter the risk reward profile. In doing this it is possible to limit risk on both the upside and downside of any trade. The use of traded options in managing risk is covered in Chapter 11, while Chapters 12–14 look at the trading method, how to select a broker and how to select a stock.

Part Three – Additional Information, concentrates on some of the more advanced aspects of options. Chapter 16 looks at the margin requirements for writing calls and puts, with corporate events covered in Chapter 17. Finally, for private investors, Chapter 18 looks at two different investment objectives and how options can be employed to achieve the desired results.

For professional users or more advanced private investors there are chapters covering advanced pricing theory, on other derivative instruments and other derivative exchanges in London.

The examples throughout the book have been given fictitious names to prevent them becoming dated too quickly. While they may have fictitious names they are all real examples. The examples do not include commission or contract charges due to the wide variation found between different stockbrokers.

At the end of each chapter there are a number of questions allowing the reader to test their understanding and retention of the main points covered. While attempting the questions is not a prerequisite for reading the book, I believe all readers will gain from the experience and should attempt them with enthusiasm. Answers to these questions can be found after Chapter 20. Some further questions relating to Parts One and Two can be found after the glossary.

I would like to acknowledge the help and support given to me by Ray Pennell, Dagmar Banton and Peter Caldwell of the London Stock Exchange, but in particular I would like to thank my wife Irene without whose encouragement the task of writing this book would have been so much harder.

Part One

THE FOUNDATIONS

1

INTRODUCTION

The view most investors have of the traded options market is one of very young traders in brightly coloured jackets, screaming and shouting at one another, waving their arms wildly. Their opinion of options as an investment is that of a high risk and ultra new instrument. This misconception can be attributed to a lack of training and education which has resulted in poor media coverage and an inaccurate view of the risks involved. Traded options, while traded by traders screaming and shouting (known as open outcry), are neither high risk nor ultra new instruments. Options allow investors to take advantage of movements in the stock market or individual shares to either speculate and make, potentially, very high returns, or insure against a possible fall in prices and thereby limit losses.

The origins of options can be traced back to ancient Greek times when, according to records, an option was taken out on olive presses. Reference has also been found in Roman documents about trading in Spanish metals. In more recent times there was an options market in Holland, on tulips, in the seventeenth century.

In 1973 the Chicago Board Options Exchange (CBOE) took a big step forward with the introduction of standard contracts and a clearing house. The clearing house serves as the ultimate counter party to all trades, allowing contracts to be opened and closed with different counter parties.

In 1978 the London Stock Exchange established the London Traded Options Market (LTOM) to trade UK equity options (in 1978 LTOM became one of only two options markets outside the US. Today every European country has its own futures and options market). Initially LTOM traded only call options on just ten stocks. The market got off to a relatively slow start, the result of a new market with a new product and the small number of stocks with options available. It was not until 1981 that put options were introduced and then not on all option stocks. The market grew steadily as both knowledge and experience spread. By March 1982 over one million contracts had changed hands, which in money terms represented over £200m. In 1983 put options were finally introduced on all stocks and 1984 saw the introduction of the FT–SE 100 share index allowing investors to take advantage of movements in the market as a whole. During 1987 more contracts were traded in a single year than in the previous nine years combined. Unfortunately the crash of 1987 knocked investors' confidence, not just in traded options but in the stock market in general, and volumes suffered accordingly.

In 1990 it was announced that LTOM and the London International Financial Futures Exchange (LIFFE) would merge into a single market. After much preparation, including the building of a new market above Cannon Street rail station, the merger took place in 1992. The new market, the largest single derivatives (futures and options) market outside the US and the third largest in the world, is known as the London International Financial Futures and Options Exchange (LIFFE). The new market now trades 70 stock options and two index options as well as financial futures and options.

Regardless of their involvement in other forms of investment, traded options have something to offer every investor from the novice with no portfolio holding to the experienced and seasoned investor with a sophisticated approach and portfolio.

Private investors generally buy call options for speculation, using their low initial outlay and high gearing to make, potentially, high gains. It is not uncommon for gains of 200–300 per cent in a matter of weeks on an outlay of a few hundred pounds. Some of the benefits of traded options are:

- Limited risk from buying options
- Potential for profits from a rising and falling market
- The ability to 'insure' a portfolio or individual stock
- A relatively small outlay for the amount of stock.

Private investors today account for 20 per cent of equity options business on LIFFE; this compares unfavourably with private investors accounting for 70–80 per cent of business in the US and Europe. This discrepancy can be attributed to the lack of education and training available for private investors, and the reluctance of some stockbrokers to enter the options market.

Changes in the taxation of traded options for pension funds and unit trusts in 1991 resulted in an increase in their use of options; however fund trustees still need persuading of the benefits. The largest two fund management companies now use options in 75 per cent of their funds.

For fund managers, options have proved to be an excellent source of additional income and a means by which it is possible to hedge a position and limit any potential loss. For stockbrokers, traded options represent an excellent opportunity to generate additional income from an existing client base.

The aim of this book is to introduce traded options to private investor and market professional alike, in a clear and concise manner. The book works through various subjects from the very basics to the advanced theories of traded options in order for it to act, not just as an introduction, but also as a reference book. Options offer one, if not the most, flexible investment vehicle available today. They can be used either to speculate and make money or to hedge a position and save money; they can be used to buy stock below the market level or sell stock above the market level. Or, for investors with a portfolio, options can increase income without the need to sell the stock. In a word they are flexible, and can be used by all to suit their own needs.

Unfortunately there are many misconceptions surrounding options, the vast majority of which are completely without foundation. Some of these misconceptions state that options are:

- Too risky for private investors
- Too complicated
- Only for professionals
- Run by and for a bunch of cowboys.

If we examine each objection in turn we can soon destroy any misconception there may be.

Options are too risky for private investors

As we will see, for a buyer of options his risk is limited to the premium paid out and is known well in advance. There are normally at least 12 exercise prices available for an investor to choose from, so even the limited risk can be adjusted to suit individual investors. Options only become risky when they are written and this should only be attempted with a full and comprehensive understanding of all the risks and rewards involved.

Options are too complicated

As with all investments, options need to be thoroughly understood before starting out. This book will explain the basic principles and terminology; the only thing left before starting to trade is to conduct 'ghost' trades to gain a feel for the market.

They are only for professionals

Traded options are not just for professionals, although in the UK professionals do, at the moment, account for the majority of business on LIFFE. In the US and in Europe 70–80 per cent of all traded options business is conducted on behalf of private investors and there is no reason why this should not be the case in the UK.

They are traded on an unregulated market

Traded options in the UK are traded on LIFFE which is a Recognised Investment Exchange (RIE). All RIEs in turn are regulated by the Securities and Investment Board (SIB) under the 1986 Financial Services Act. LIFFE is the largest derivatives' exchange in Europe and cannot afford not to regulate its markets to the highest level.

Besides the exchange being regulated, all traders are authorised as fit and proper people to trade by the Securities and Futures Authority (SFA). LIFFE is a well-run and well-regulated market.

Having dispelled some of the misconceptions surrounding traded options and very briefly discussed some of the benefits, I hope the reader is encouraged to read on and by the end of the book, armed with the relevant information, knowledgeable enough to enter the options market as part of their investment strategy.

2

BASIC CONCEPT AND TERMINOLOGY

BASIC CONCEPT

What is an option?

Traded options, as with most forms of investment, are surrounded by mystery and their own unique terminology. It is important to break through the mystery and understand the terminology as early as possible in order to get a clear and concise picture of traded options. Once we have broken through we can begin to see what options are and how they can be used. Along with the basic concept of traded options this chapter will explain the terminology in clear and concise terms.

To understand the basic concept we will move away from stocks and shares for a moment and have a look at something we can all relate to in everyday life, buying a car.

An investor decides he wants to buy a new car. He goes along to a garage and after careful consideration places a deposit on the car. The deposit specifies that he is buying a car, or a number of cars, the make and model, the cost of each car, the amount of deposit and how long the deposit is valid for. Once he has paid his deposit the investor has secured the purchase price of the car, regardless of what happens elsewhere in the car market or the economy. There are two choices he can now make about what to do with his deposit. He can:

1 Take up his deposit and buy the car.
2 Do nothing and lose his deposit.

The deposit giving the right to purchase the car is the same as a traded option on a company's shares. A traded option is simply a method of securing either a purchase or sale price of shares.

After careful consideration an investor decides he wishes to purchase an option. He approaches his broker and places his order. The price will depend on the type of option it is and the purchase or sale price it secures.

Each option specifies what type of option it is (to buy or sell the shares); the number of shares involved (the contract specifications); name and type of shares (the underlying security); the purchase or sale price (the exercise/strike price); the amount of deposit (cost or premium of the option)and finally how long it is valid for (its expiry date).

Once the option has been purchased, the holder has the same choices to make, about the option, as the investor with the deposit on the car. He can:

1 Take up his deposit and buy the shares (this is known as *to exercise the option*).
2 Do nothing and lose his deposit (known as *to abandon the option*).

However, a traded option is a security in its own right and may be bought or sold in the market at any time during its life. The option's price will fluctuate as the price of the underlying security (the shares the option is based on, i.e. BT) moves up or down. This means the holder of a traded option has a third choice, to sell the option back into the market for a profit. The vast majority of investors trade their options back into the market, rather than exercise or abandon them.

Option trading is a form of certificateless trading. No certificates are issued by company registrars. Instead, evidence of ownership is via a contract note issued by brokers (Fig. 2.1). In addition, records of ownership are maintained by the London Clearing House.

TERMINOLOGY

Before we go on, we need to look at the formal definition of an option and some of the terminology used. The definition of a traded option states:

An option is an agreement between a buyer (holder) and a seller (writer) giving the buyer the right, but not the obligation, to buy (call) or sell (put)

Subject to the rules and regulations of the London International Financial Futures and Options Exchange.

Client Reference:
Bargain/Tax Date:

Bargain Reference:
Settlement Date:

Thank you for your instructions and have sold to you as principal

BOOTS CO / JAN 94 / 550 / CALL OPTIONS

You have bought to open:

Time	Quantity	Price	Consideration
09 38	5	7	350.00

Consideration	350.00
Commission	20.00
VAT at 17.5%	NIL
Contract Charges	7.50
Total	377.50

Figure 2.1 Contract note

an asset on or before a given date, at a specified price in return for a consideration.

The easiest way to understand this definition is to break it down into its component parts and look at each one individually.

The *holder* of the option has purchased the right to buy or sell shares in the underlying security. A *writer* of an option is on the opposite side of this trade and has sold the right. He now has an obligation linked to the holder's rights and must either buy or sell the underlying security if exercised against.

The holder has *the right, but not the obligation* to buy or sell; the holder can choose what to do with the option, just like the investor with the deposit on the car; exercise it, sell it back into the market or abandon it. The seller has no rights, but he does have an obligation and must wait to see what the holder wishes to do with his option. If the holder does exercise his right to buy or sell the shares, the writer must either sell the shares to the holder or buy them from him.

There are two types or classes of option; *calls* and *puts*. A call option gives the holder the right to purchase shares in the underlying security if the option is exercised. A put option gives the holder the right to sell shares in the underlying security if the option is exercised. The writer of a call option has no rights but is obliged to sell (deliver) the shares, to the holder, if exercised against. The writer of a put option, again has no rights, but must buy (take delivery) of the stock, from the holder, if exercised against.

An *asset* is the security the option is based on. It is usually called the underlying security.

On or before a given date. Options have a limited life. The maximum life of an equity option is nine months from the date of its introduction. When options are first introduced, they are allocated to one of three expiry cycles. Which cycle they are allocated to will depend on when the company's results are announced. The three cycles are:

1	Jan	April	July	Oct
2	Feb	May	Aug	Nov
3	Mar	June	Sept	Dec

The nearest or closest three expiry months, within each cycle, to today's date are always in existence. Once the nearest expiry date passes, the next in the sequence is introduced to maintain three expiry dates, at three-month intervals, in each cycle.

50	140	330	700	1150
60	160	360	750	1200
70	180	390	800	1250
80	200	420	850	1300
90	220	460	900	1350
100	240	500	950	1400
110	260	550	1000	1450
120	280	600	1050	1500
130	300	650	1100	1600

Table 2.1 Exercise prices

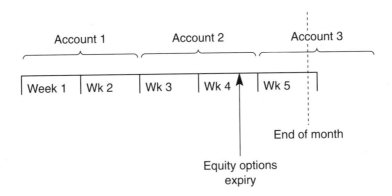

Figure 2.2 Equity options expiry date

The expiry date of an option can be calculated by looking for the last Wednesday in the last full stock exchange account period in the expiry month (Fig. 2.2).

The specific price is the price at which the shares in the underlying security may be bought or sold by the holder if the option is exercised, and is known as the exercise or strike price. These prices are set by the exchange according to a fixed table (Table 2.1) depending on the underlying security share price.

When an option is introduced to the market, whether it is due to the expiry of an old option or being introduced for the first time, there will always be two exercise prices above and below the market price of the shares. In addition, if the underlying security price is the same as or near to an exercise price, that exercise price will be introduced with the next two exercise prices in the sequence above and below. During the life of the option it may be necessary to introduce new exercise prices if the price of the underlying security rises or falls. If the market price of the underlying security falls below the second lowest exercise price, or rises above the second highest exercise price the next exercise price in the price table (Table 2.1) will be introduced. New exercise prices may also be introduced, at the discretion of the market officials, if the market traders request their introduction to aid trading in any way.

The *consideration* is the cost of the option and is known as the *premium*. Premiums for UK equity options are expressed in pence per share. The premium is paid by the buyer (holder) to the seller (writer). It represents the maximum loss for a buyer (holder) and the maximum profit for a seller (writer).

Traded options are traded in *contracts*, with each contract normally representing 1000 shares. To determine the cost of a contract the premium is multiplied by the contract size (24p × 1000 = £240). Dealing is only permitted in whole contracts, no fractions of contracts are allowed. Changes to contract specifications are sometimes made to reflect changes in the underlying security, e.g. rights issue or capitalisation issue. These changes are covered in greater depth later in the book. When describing options it is usual to include four pieces of information:

1 The underlying security.
2 The expiry date.
3 Exercise price.
4 Type of option (call or put).

For example, 'ABC Jan 390 call'. This information and description are known as a series. All options with the same underlying security, expiry date, exercise price and pertaining to the same class, belong to the same series.

An investor who opens or increases his position by buying options is transacting an *opening purchase* and becomes the holder of options. When he sells some or all of his holding he is closing his position and is transacting a *closing sale*.

An investor who opens or increases his position by selling options is transacting an *opening sale* and becomes the writer of options. When he buys back some or all of the options he has written, thereby extinguishing his obligations, he is transacting a *closing purchase*.

Example 1 is a brief description of how a call traded option works.

Example 1

It is mid August and an investor buys a Nov 460 call option on ABC shares for 8p. Excluding commission charges the option will cost £80 (8p per share x 1000 as there are normally 1000 shares per contract).

This gives the investor the right, if he chooses, to purchase 1000 ABC shares at 460. The investor may do this any time prior to the option's expiry date in November. If the value of ABC shares rises before November, to say 490, the right to buy at 460 (the exercise price) will be worth at least 30 (the difference between the option's exercise price and the price of the shares in the market). The investor now has two choices to make. **1** Use the option and buy the shares, or **2** sell the option back into the market.

1 If the investor decides to exercise his option, he can purchase the shares at 460 (exercise price) using his option and sell immediately at 490 in the stock market. This will realise an instant profit of £220 excluding commission charges.

Exercise price	460
Cost of option	8
Purchase price of shares	468
Sale price in market	490
Profit	22 per share × 1000

2 If the investor sells his option back into the market the price of the option will be at least 30 and may be more, say 34. (With the market price for BT shares being 490, having the right to buy at 460 is worth at least 30.) By selling the option back into the market the investor will make a profit of £260 excluding commission charges.

Cost of option	8
Sale price of option	34
Profit	26 per share × 1000

Using traded options a profit of £260 has resulted from an initial outlay of £80, a gain of 325 per cent.

Example 1 gave a brief description of a traded option and the terminology used. As you progress through the book the concept of options and how and why they work will be explained in greater depth. The

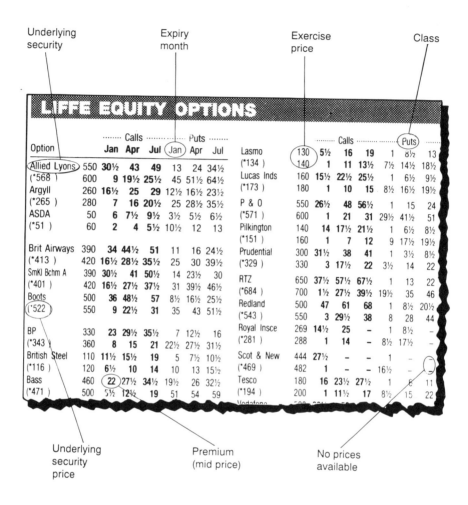

Figure 2.3 Option prices in the FT

prices of traded options are published daily in all quality newspapers such as the *Financial Times* and are usually set out as in Fig. 2.3.

Prices can also be found on BBC 2 CEEFAX or it is possible to purchase information systems such as Market Eye or Topic although these are quite expensive.

REVISION QUESTIONS – CHAPTER 2

Questions are in the form of statements which are either true or false; circle T or F to indicate your answer. Answers can be found after Chapter 20.

1 There are two types or classes of options, calls and puts.   T F

2 The holder of a call option can sell the underlying security at the exercise price.   T F

3 The premium of an option is its cost expressed in pence per share.   T F

4 The exercise price of an option is the price per share at which the holder can buy or sell the underlying security.   T F

5 The maximum life of an option is six months.   T F

6 If an investor purchases an option with a premium of 18p, this represents the maximum loss the investor can incur.   T F

7 There are normally 1500 shares in one option's contract.   T F

8 The underlying security of an option is the company's shares the option is based on.   T F

9 There are two expiry cycles that a traded option can be allocated to.   T F

10 The holder of an option may sell it back into the market any time during the options life.   T F

3

BASIC TRADES

There are many possible trades and strategies with traded options. Some have weird and wonderful names, such as butterfly, condor and strangles, but no matter how complicated they may appear to be, they are all made up of a combination of four basic trades. Before looking at the more complicated and exotic trades it is necessary to have a good understanding of the basics. (During the coming chapters buying may also be referred to as being long and writing may be referred to as being short.)

1 BUYING (LONG) CALLS

Call options give the holder the right to buy the underlying security and are usually purchased in the expectation of a rise in the value of the underlying security. This rise will result in an increase in the value of option which may then be either exercised and the underlying security purchased or the option sold back into the market at a profit.

Example 1

It is the beginning of August and the share price of ABC Ltd is 290. An investor takes a view that the share price is about to rise over the next few weeks. He buys one Oct 300 call option for 14p. The option gives the investor the right to purchase ABC Ltd shares at 300 (exercise price) any time during the life of the option. The cost of the option, excluding commission charges, is £140 (premium × contract size, 14p × 1000 = £140). If the share price increases before the expiry of the option, to say 320, the option will also have increased in value, to possibly 28. Having the right to buy something valued at 320 for 300 must be worth at least 20 and with there being time left until the expiry of the option its premium will be higher. The holder is now able to sell the option, realising 100 per cent profit without owning the shares.

	Option's market	**Stock market**
Aug Share price 290	Buy one Oct 300 call option at 14 (£140)	Buy 1000 ABC Ltd shares at 290 (£2900)
Oct Share price 320	Sell one Oct 300 call option at 28 (£280)	Sell 1000 ABC Ltd shares at 320 (£3200)
Profit	14 (£140) or 100%	30 (£300) or 10.3%

The potential profit or loss of any option position can be illustrated by a simple graph. The graph shows the possible profit or loss, of an option, *at expiry*, for any given price of the underlying security. The profit and loss profile for Example 1 is shown in Fig. 3.1. On the vertical axis is the profit or loss for the position and on the horizontal axis is the underlying security price.

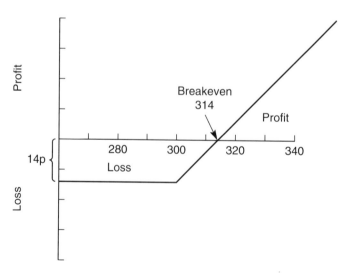

Figure 3.1 Long 300 call option

Figure 3.1 shows that while the underlying security's price is at or below 300 (exercise price) at expiry, the position is looking at a loss equal to the premium paid, 14p. Once the underlying security price rises above 300, every penny rise will eat into the loss by a penny, until the position breaks even at 314 (exercise price + premium). After the break-even point, every penny rise in the underlying security will result in a penny rise in the profit. The maximum loss is limited to the premium paid while the maximum profit is unlimited.

Advantages of a long call

- **Limited loss**. The maximum loss with a long call position is limited to the premium paid for the option.
- **Unlimited profit**. The profit potential for a long call is unlimited with the underlying security price being free to rise as far as the market will allow.
- **Limited outlay**. The premium paid for the option is a fraction of the cost of acquiring control over the same amount of stock, allowing the remainder to be invested elsewhere.
- **Gearing**. It is possible to make considerable gains in the option's premium for a relatively small movement in the underlying security price.

Disadvantage

- **Time**. The passage of time works against the time value part of the option's premium.

2 WRITING (SHORT) CALLS

A writer of a call option is obliged to sell or deliver the underlying security if called upon to do so. Call options are generally written in the expectation of the underlying security price remaining stable or falling slightly. This will result in the buyer of the option not wishing to exercise his option, allowing the writer to keep the premium received. This premium represents the maximum profit a writer can make.

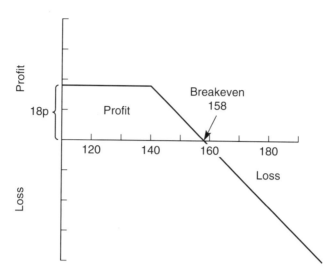

Figure 3.2 Short 140 call option

Example 2

It is early August and the share price of XYZ Plc is 152. An investor takes a view that the share price will remain stable or possibly fall slightly over the coming months. To take advantage of this situation he decides to write a Nov 140 call option for 18. The writer will receive £180 (premium × contract size). The option gives the writer no rights, but he is obliged to deliver stock at the exercise price of 140 if exercised against. The share price falls to 138. The holder of a 140 call option will not normally exercise a 140 call option with the market price of the underlying security at 138 (he will not wish to buy something at 140 if he can buy it at 138 elsewhere). This will allow the writer to keep the premium as profit. Most cases of options being exercised occur near to or at expiry.

The profit and loss profile for a short call position is illustrated in Fig. 3.2. When selling a 140 call option for 18 the writer receives the premium and this represents the maximum profit he can make. The writer will only make this profit if the underlying security price is at 140 or below at expiry and the option remains unexercised. The break-even point for the trade is 158 (exercise price + premium). The writer is looking at, potentially, an unlimited loss if the underlying security price continues to rise above the break-even point and the writer is exercised against.

The writer may close out his position, thereby extinguishing his liabilities, at any time by purchasing an option identical to the one he has sold (same exercise price, expiry date and underlying security).

Advantages of a short call

- **Premium received**. The premium received generates additional income and earnings.
- **Time**. The passage of time works to the advantage of the writer of call options.

Disadvantages

- **Exercise**. The option may be exercised against the writer, forcing him to deliver the underlying security at a price below the current market level.
- **Unlimited loss**. If the underlying security price rises above the break-even point, the writer of the call is looking at, potentially, an unlimited loss.

Call writers fall into one of two categories, covered or uncovered (naked). Covered call writers hold the underlying security to cover the possibility of being exercised against. If they are assigned they can deliver the stock without having to purchase it in the equity market, at a level above the exercise price. Uncovered or naked writers do not hold the underlying security. If exercised against they must purchase stock in the equity market at the current level which will be above the exercise price of the option. If the current market level is constantly rising, the uncovered writer is facing a potentially unlimited loss. Writing uncovered calls can be extremely risky (costly) and should only be considered if the investor is confident he understands all the risks involved and is an experienced options investor.

To ensure the writer can perform his contractual obligations and sell the underlying security if exercised against, he must lodge margin with his broker. Margin, in the form of cash or securities, acts as a form of insurance to ensure that he can perform his contractual obligations and is returned to the writer once the position has been closed and his obligations extinguished. Margin is discussed in more detail later in the book.

3 BUYING (LONG) PUTS

Put options allow the holder to sell the underlying security if he wishes and are usually purchased in the expectation of a substantial fall in the underlying security price. The fall in the value of the underlying security will result in an increase in the value of the option. Once the option has increased in value it may be either exercised and the stock sold or the option may be sold back into the market at a profit.

Example 3

It is 1 Sept and XYZ Plc shares are trading at 260. An investor anticipates that the price will fall substantially in the coming weeks and so purchases a Feb 280 put with a premium of 36. The option gives the holder the right to sell XYZ Plc shares any time during the life of the option for 280 (exercise price). The cost of the option is £360 (premium × contract size). If before the expiry of the option the underlying security price falls, to say 230, the value of the option will be at least 50 (the intrinsic value of the option). But, with there still being time until expiry, the option's premium may be more, say 53. The investor can now either exercise the option and sell stock at 280 or sell the option back into the market for a profit at 53.

As with all option trades it is not necessary to hold stock in order to trade in options.

The profit and loss profile (Fig. 3.3) shows the position at expiry for the trade in Example 3. If the underlying security price is above 280 (exercise price) at expiry the holder will lose the premium (36) paid out. As the stock falls the holder's loss will be eroded until the trade breaks even at 244 (exercise price–premium). If the stock continues to fall, the holder has a potentially unlimited profit.

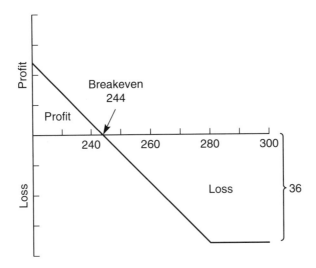

Figure 3.3 Long 280 put option

Advantages of a long put

- **Profit from falling market**. A put option allows an investor to profit from a falling market without going short of the stock.
- **Limited loss**. The maximum loss with a long put is limited to the premium paid out.
- **Unlimited profit**. The profit potential is limited only by the fact that the furthest the underlying security price can fall to is zero.
- **Gearing**. It is possible to make considerable gains for a relatively small fall in the underlying security.

Disadvantages

- **Time**. The passage of time works against the time value element of the option's premium and in favour of the writer.

4 WRITING (SHORT) PUTS

Put options are usually written when expecting the underlying security to either remain stable or rising slightly. This will enable the

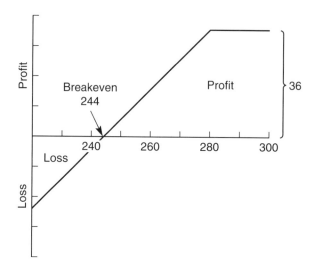

Figure 3.4 Short 280 put option

writer to retain the option's premium received as profit due to the holder not wishing to exercise his option.

Example 4

Mega Bucks Ltd stock is trading at 276 and an investor believes the stock will rise slightly over the next month but not enough to warrant the purchase of call options. To take advantage of this situation he decides to write a Dec 280 put for 36. As the writer of an option he receives the premium of 36 (£360 , premium × contract size). The writer has no rights, but is obliged to take delivery of (buy) the stock if exercised against. Over the next month the stock rises to 283. The holder of the Dec 280 put has the right to sell stock at 280 (exercise price), but will not do so if he can sell stock in the market at 283. This will enable the writer to keep the premium received as profit.

The profit and loss profile (Fig. 3.4) shows the writer has sold the 280 put for a premium of 36. The premium is the maximum profit that can be made, but only as long as the share price stays above 280. Below 280 for every penny fall in the share price the writer will lose one penny of premium, breaking even at 244 (exercise price–premium). If the share price continues to fall below 244 the writer will make a penny loss for every penny fall. This loss is limited by the fact that the underlying security price can only fall to zero.

Advantages of a short put

- **Premium received**. The premium received generates additional earnings.
- **Time**. The passage of time works in favour of the writer.

Disadvantages

- **Unlimited loss**. The potential loss for a short put is unlimited if the underlying security price falls.
- **Exercise**. The writer of a short put may be exercised against forcing him to take delivery of stock above the current market price.

WHAT AND WHEN TO BUY OR SELL

As we have seen, when and what to buy or sell will depend on the investor's expectations and how much risk he is willing to accept.

If the investor is bullish about the underlying security, he should consider buying call options. If the expectation is slightly bullish or neutral, the investor should write (sell) puts.

With a bearish outlook the investor should buy puts. If the assumption is a slightly bearish or neutral one, writing (selling) calls would be appropriate.

No matter what the expectation is, the degree of risk with each trade can be adjusted to suit each individual investor by altering the series bought or sold. This is covered more fully in the chapters on gearing and buying and selling calls and puts.

Until you are absolutely certain that you understand options and all the risks involved it is suggested that you concentrate on buying (holding) call and put options.

Outlook	Trade
Bullish	Buy calls
Neutral/slightly bullish	Write (sell) puts
Bearish	Buy puts
Neutral/slightly bearish	Write (sell) calls

The effect of the erosion of time value cannot be stressed too highly. It is important when buying traded options not only to correctly anticipate the direction of any price movement, but also the extent and period involved. With so many series available (there will always be a minimum of 12 in both calls and puts) the choice can seem bewildering.

The main factor in making this choice is the underlying security; is it going to move and if so how far? How soon and in which direction? When purchasing the underlying security as an investment it is not necessary to know how far or how fast the stock will move as there is no time limit on the stock. However, with options being a wasting asset and each passing day eroding the value, timing is as important as picking the right direction.

A short, sharp movement in the underlying security will produce spectacular gains in the short-dated out-of-the-money series due to the gearing effect. However, if the investor gets the timing of the rise (fall) wrong there is an increased chance (almost a certainty) that the investor will lose all of his investment as the premium, being made up entirely of time value, will erode at a spectacular rate.

If the rise (fall) in the underlying security is expected over the medium term, then the investor has the choice of either short-dated (near month) in-the-money options or using the longer dated (far month) series. The choice is entirely dependent on the timing of the rise (fall). If the rise (fall) is expected to continue after the expiry of the short date near month, then the longer dated options should be purchased.

Purchasing in-the-money options is often thought of as being a more conservative approach to options trading. With their premium being made up of intrinsic value and time value, the possibility of losing the entire premium if the expected rise (fall) does not materi-

Position	Risk	Reward
Long Call	Premium paid	Unlimited
Short Call	Unlimited	Premium received
Long Put	Premium paid	Unlimited
Short Put	Unlimited	Premium received

Table 3.1 Risk reward

alise is much reduced. But with in-the-money options premium being more expensive due to intrinsic value, if the investor's expectations prove to be completely false and the stock falls (rises), he could lose considerably more than an investor with an out-of-the-money buyer.

Most trading takes place in the near-dated out-of-the-money options with investors looking for highly geared results. Longer dated months are less susceptible to small fluctuations in volatility and adverse movements in the underlying security than the short-dated expiry months and should not be ruled out by investors.

Table 3.1 is a summary of risk reward potential for the four basic trades. All investors should be fully conversant with this before trading. The risk and rewards can be altered to suit any situation as we shall see in later chapters.

REVISION QUESTIONS – CHAPTER 3

Questions 1–3 refer to the following trade. An investor purchases one Nov 180 call for 12p with the underlying security at 188.

1 The maximum loss for the buyer of the Nov 180 call is 12p. T F

2 The break-even point for the trade is 168. T F

3 The maximum profit is the premium 12p. T F

4 The disadvantages with a short call are the potential for unlimited loss and the possibility of being exercised against. T F

5 If an investor considers the market is about to rise he should buy put options. T F

6 The maximum profit for a short call position is unlimited. T F

7 If exercised against the seller of a call must deliver the underlying security at the exercise price. T F

8 When exercised against the writer of a put must deliver the underlying security. T F

9 Call options are usually purchased when the underlying security is expected to rise. T F

10 Put options are usually purchased when anticipating a fall in the price of the underlying security. T F

4

INDEX OPTIONS

In addition to UK equity options LIFFE trade options based on the *Financial Times* – Stock Exchange 100 share index (FT–SE 100, also known as the footsie). The index was introduced, specifically for futures and options, in 1984 and consists of the top 100 listed UK companies by market capitalisation. This is calculated by multiplying the company's share price by the number of its shares in existence. The market capitalisation of the constituents of the index and all other shares on the stock market are reviewed quarterly and changes made to the membership of the index if necessary.

The index is arithmetically weighted, i.e. more value is given to a 1p movement in the shares of some companies than for a 1p movement in other companies' shares. This ensures a company's market capitalisation is taken into consideration when calculating movements in the index. The value of the index is calculated every minute by the London Stock Exchange using the share prices quoted on SEAQ (the share dealing system) and the arithmetical formula and therefore acts as a real-time indicator to the level of the UK stock market. The base was set at 1000.0 on 31 December 1983.

The FT–SE 100 option is what is known as a contract for difference. If exercised there is no delivery or receipt of actual stock. Instead the option is settled for cash. The amount of cash received or paid being calculated by the difference between the exercise price and the index value when exercised (known as the Exchange Delivery Settlement Price) × £10.

There are two styles of index options: European and American. European options can only be exercised at expiry, whereas American options can be exercised at any time, on any business day during the life of the option. All equity options are American style options; however they may not be exercised on the last day of a stock exchange account period.

Unlike equity options, where there are three expiry dates with three months between each date, index options have their own different expiry cycles. American style index options (Example 1) expiry dates are the closest four months to today's date, plus June and December. This cycle gives the index a maximum life of 12 months. European style index options (Example 2) have March, June, September and December, plus the two nearest months.

Example 1

It is 1 Jan and the expiry dates for the American style index options are:

Jan, Feb, Mar, Apr (being the closest four months) plus June and Dec.

When Jan expires, May will be introduced. When Feb expires, there will be no new month introduced as June is already in existence.

When June is the closest month and about to expire, the sequence will be June, July, Aug, Sept + Dec. When June does expire, Oct will be introduced along with a 12 month June date.

Example 2

It is 1 Jan and the expiry dates available for the European style index options are:

Jan, Feb (being the two closest months to today's date) plus March, Jun, Sept and Dec.

When Jan expires, April will be introduced, still giving the four standard expiry months, plus the two additional near months. When Feb expires, May will be introduced as the second additional near-dated expiry month. When March expires, March the following year will be the new month introduced to maintain the four standard expiry months. No new near-dated expiry month will be introduced.

The FT–SE 100 expires at 10.30 a.m. on the third Friday of the expiry month. The value of the index is recorded every minute from 10.10 to 10.30. The three highest and lowest readings are discarded

Time	Index level	Time	Index level
10.10	3198.4	10.21	3195.6†
10.11	3199.1*	10.22	3197.8
10.12	3198.2	10.23	3197.5
10.13	3197.6	10.24	3198.1
10.14	3198.3	10.25	3197.2
10.15	3197.2	10.26	3198.8
10.16	3196.8	10.27	3198.7
10.17	3195.0†	10.28	3198.9*
10.18	3194.9†	10.29	3198.4
10.19	3195.8	10.30	3199.3*
10.20	3196.7		

Table 4.1 Index expiry

Exchange Delivery Settlement Price = 3197.7

* three highest readings
† three lowest readings

and the average taken from the remaining 15 readings (Table 4.1). The expiry level is known as the Exchange Delivery Settlement Price.

The settlement price of the footsie is calculated in this manner to prevent any large investment houses from manipulating the index to their advantage and profit.

The FT–SE 100 can be used for both speculative and hedging purposes. Hedging, a type of insurance, compensates a fall in the value of the portfolio with a rise in the value of the option.

Example 3 (speculative)

Imagine it is 1 May and the index stands at 2860. This represents £28,600 (the index value × £10).

An investor buys a June 2850 call for 75. This gives the holder the right to purchase the index value at the close of business on the day of exercise for £28,500.

In June, just before expiry, the index is valued at 2935 (or £29,350). The holder of the June 2850 call has the choice to either exercise the option and purchase the index or sell the option back into the market for its premium. By exercising the option and buying the index at 2935 the investor will make £850 profit (purchase £29,350 for £28,500). Selling the option back into the market, the investor will receive the premium, which may be 87 or £870 profit.

Example 4 (hedging)

An investor has a portfolio of shares valued at £300,000. The calculation for designing the necessary hedge is as follows:

$$\frac{\text{Value of portfolio}}{\text{Index} \times £10} = \text{number of contracts}$$

With the index standing at say 3000 the hedge is:

$$\frac{£300,000}{3000 \times 10} = 10$$

The put option purchased will depend on the amount of protection the investor requires. A near-dated option will provide short-term protection, while a longer dated option will provide long-term protection. However, long-term protection will cost more than short-term protection. The exercise price chosen will also affect the level of protection.

% Change	FT–SE level	Portfolio value £	Put option profit/ loss	Portfolio value £
–20%	2400	240,000	+57,500	297,500
–10%	2700	270,000	+27,500	297,500
level	3000	300,000	–2,500	297,500
+10%	3300	330,000	–2,500	327,500
+20%	3600	360,000	–2,500	357,500

Table 4.2 Hedged portfolio

A higher exercise price will result in a higher level of protection but will also cost more. In this example the investor purchases ten Dec 3000 put options with a premium of 25. The hedge will cost £2500 plus commission to establish.

As the index and the value of the portfolio falls the value of the put option rises to cover the loss, ensuring that the value of the portfolio does not fall below £297,500 (Table 4.2). If the index does not fall as anticipated but in fact rises, the value of the portfolio will still increase in value but, at a reduced rate equal to the premium paid for the put position. The puts do not have to be kept until expiry but can be sold for their premium at any time that they are no longer required.

REVISION QUESTIONS – CHAPTER 4

1 Index options are based on the FT all share index.   T F
2 Inclusion in the index depends on a company's market   T F
  capitalisation.
3 The index is cash settled if exercised.   T F
4 Each index point is worth £25.   T F
5 European style options can be exercised at any time   T F
  during their life.

Part Two

TRADING

5

PRICING TRADED OPTIONS

To understand how and why different events have different effects on options premiums and how and why different strategies work, it is necessary to understand the principles of pricing traded options.

OPTIONS PRICING VARIABLES

There are six main variables used in calculating the fair value of an options premium:

- Stock price
- Exercise price
- Time to expiry
- Volatility
- Dividends
- Interest rates.

Intrinsic value

The first two variables (stock price and exercise price) determine intrinsic and time values. The premium or cost of an option is made up of two elements, intrinsic value and time value.

PREMIUM = INTRINSIC VALUE + TIME VALUE

Intrinsic value is the real or tangible value of an option.

Underlying security: 345. Option: Jan 330 call option. Having the right to buy something worth 345 for 330 is worth at least 15. This is the real or intrinsic value of an option.

$$\text{underlying security price} - \text{exercise price} =$$
$$\text{intrinsic value}$$
$$345 - 330 = 15$$

For a call option to have intrinsic value its exercise price must be below the underlying security price. This gives the holder the right to buy the underlying security at a price below the current market level.

Call intrinsic value = underlying security price − exercise price

Put options have intrinsic value when their exercise price is above the current market price of the underlying security. This will allow the holder to sell the underlying security above the market level.

Put intrinsic value = exercise price − underlying security price

If we now look at the prices in Table 5.1, the 220 call option gives the holder the right to buy the underlying security at 220. With the share price at 247, the 220 call option has an intrinsic value of 27, the difference (or profit) between the exercise price and the current underlying security price. The 240 call option has an intrinsic value of 7, the difference between the exercise price and the underlying security. The 260 and 280 call options have no intrinsic value as their exercise prices are 13 and 33 over the current share price respectively.

	Share price 247			
Exercise price	Call		Put	
	Intrinsic value	Premium	Intrinsic value	Premium
220	27	33	0	3
240	7	18	0	8
260	0	8	13	19
280	0	4	33	36

Table 5.1 Intrinsic value

	Share price 606			
Exercise price	*Call options*			
	Dec	Mar	Jun	
550	59	67	74	In-the-money
600	19	32	42	At-the-money
650	3	13	20	Out-of-the-money
Exercise price	*Put options*			
	Dec	Mar	Jun	
550	1	6	9	Out-of-the-money
600	10	22	26	At-the-money
650	45	53	5	In-the-money

Table 5.2 In-, out-and at-the-money

If we look at the puts, the 220 and 240 puts have no intrinsic value as their exercise prices are below the current market price of the under-lying security. (Don't forget puts give the holder the right to sell and therefore the exercise price needs to be above the market price to make a profit.) With the share price at 247 the 260 puts have an intrinsic value of 13 and the 280 put has an intrinsic value of 33.

Any option with intrinsic value is known as *in-the-money* (Table 5.2). Any option with no intrinsic value is known as *out-of-the-money*. An option with an exercise price equal to the underlying security price is known as *at-the-money*.

Time value

If the intrinsic value of an option is subtracted from its premium the figure remaining is known as time value. Time value represents the remaining life of an option and the possibility of price movements in

	Share price 247					
Exercise price	Call			Put		
	Intrinsic value	Premium	Time value	Intrinsic value	Premium	Time value
220	27 —— 33 ——		6	0 —— 3 ——		3
240	7 —— 18 ——		11	0 —— 8 ——		8
260	0 —— 8 ——		8	13 —— 19 ——		6
280	0 —— 4 ——		4	33 —— 36 ——		3

Table 5.3 Time value

the underlying security and subsequently the option's premium, before expiry. The longer an option has until it expires the greater its time value will be due to the increased opportunity for price movements in the underlying security price. As the option moves closer to expiry so its time value will erode at an ever increasing rate. Initially, this erosion will be slow and almost undetectable but, as the option approaches expiry, time value will erode at an ever increasing rate. Approximately 60 per cent of time value erodes in the last 30 per cent of an option's life span.

If we look at Table 5.3 we know the 220 call has 27 intrinsic value which, when subtracted from its premium of 33, gives a time value of 6. The 240 call with an intrinsic value of 7 leaves a time value of 11. The 260 and 280 calls have no intrinsic value, so their whole premium is made up of time value.

With the puts the 220 and 240 puts have no intrinsic value and their premiums represent just time value. The 260 put has 13 intrinsic value leaving a time value element of 6 and finally the 280 put has an intrinsic value of 33 leaving 3 time value.

We can see from this example that time value is greatest when an option is at-the-money (exercise price closest to underlying security price) and decreases the further the option becomes either into or out-of-the-money. The reason for this increase of time value when an

Underlying security price 410			
Exercise price	Feb	May	Aug
420	2	18	28

Table 5.4 Time value increase

option is at-the-money is uncertainty. The deeper an option is in-the-money the greater the probability of it expiring in-the-money. The deeper an option is out-of-the-money the greater the probability of it expiring out-of-the-money. However when an option is at-the-money it is possible for the option to move into or out-of-the-money. The extra time value is to compensate the writer for this uncertainty.

Time value can be thought of as a type of insurance, against the possible price movement of the underlying security, that is payable by the buyer to the seller (writer) of an option. As with all insurance policies the longer the insurance is to run for, the higher the premium paid (12 months car insurance policy will be more expensive than a 6 months policy).

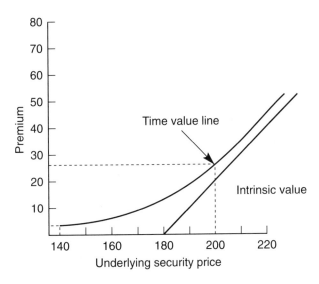

Figure 5.1 Time value

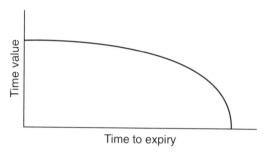

Figure 5.2 Time value decay

Table 5.4 shows how the premium of options with the same exercise price increases when the life of the option is increased.

The time value element of any option can be plotted on a graph (Fig 5.1). The graph shows that when an option is at-the-money the time value element of its premium is at its greatest. This is due to the uncertainty of whether the option will move into or out-of-the-money.

The graph shows the premium make-up for a 180 call option. If the underlying security price is at 140 the premium is made up entirely of time value. The same is true when the underlying security price is at 160, although the time value has now increased in recognition that the option is moving towards gaining intrinsic value.

When the underlying security is at 200 the 180 call premium is made up of 20 intrinsic value plus time value. As the option goes further into the money so time value diminishes. This is due to the near certainty that the option will expire in-the-money.

Time to expiry

As an option approaches expiry so its time value erodes. To begin with this erosion is slow and almost unnoticeable due to the length of the life of the option, but as the option draws nearer to expiry, so the erosion of time value increases. The decrease in time value continues at an ever increasing rate until, on expiry, there is no time value left and the option's premium is made up entirely of its intrinsic value (Fig 5.2).

This erosion of time value works against holders of options and in favour of writers. Erosion of time value cannot be stressed too highly and must be considered by all holders of options.

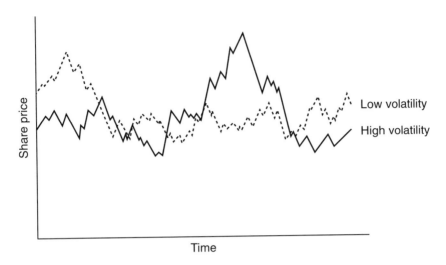

Figure 5.3 Volatility

During the life of an option an in-the-money option's premium comprises of its intrinsic and time value, an out-of-the-money option has no intrinsic value so its premium will be made up entirely of time value. At expiry an in-the-money option's premium will comprise entirely of its intrinsic value and an out-of-the-money option's premium will be zero. This is because at expiry there is no time left for an option to gain intrinsic or tangible value, an out-of-the-money option is worthless.

Volatility

Volatility is a measure of the movement of a share's price over a given time (Fig. 5.3). The greater the price movements of an underlying security, the greater the possibility of the option gaining intrinsic value and expiring in-the-money. If an underlying security has a high volatility a buyer of the option can expect to pay more for it than for an option on a stock with low volatility.

Types of volatility

There are several different ways of measuring volatility:

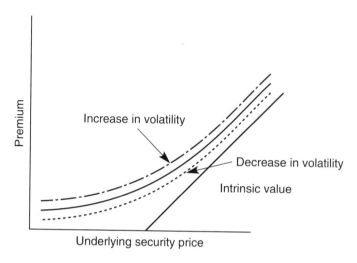

Figure 5.4 Changes in volatility

- *Historic volatility* looks at the past performance of the underlying security. It is known and can be easily measured. However, past performance is no guarantee of future performance.
- *Forecast volatility* tries to anticipate what will happen in the future and is, by its very nature, not an exact science.
- *Implied volatility* is the volatility implicit in the prices being traded today.
- *Future volatility* is the one every one wants to know.

As with time value, volatility can be plotted on a graph. Figure 5.4 shows the effect of an increase and a decrease in volatility.

An increase in volatility will increase premiums, due to the additional uncertainty of the underlying security's price movements. The increased price movements will affect the option's chance of expiring in-the-money. A decrease in volatility will result in a decrease in premiums as the chance of an option expiring in-the-money has diminished.

Dividends

Holders of traded options are not entitled to any dividends paid on the underlying security and therefore dividends have no DIRECT effect

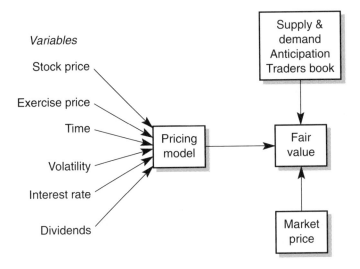

Figure 5.5 Option pricing models

on premiums. However, dividend payments are gradually built into the price of the underlying security. On ex date (the last date on which buyers of the underlying security will appear on the share register and therefore receive the dividend) the underlying security price will be reduced by the amount of the dividend payment. This reduction will affect the option's premiums and result in call prices being reduced and put prices increased. The underlying security is usually marked ex-dividend on the first day of dealing of a new stock exchange account period. Traded options however cannot be exercised on the last day of an account period and are therefore treated as being marked ex-dividend on the last but one day of dealing on the previous account (usually a Thursday). Dividend dates and expected payments are usually forecast well in advance and should therefore be built into any prices and strategies used.

Interest rates

Interest rates have a bearing on options premiums when calculating what is known as the *cost of carry*. This is a complicated formula for calculating the cost of borrowing money and purchasing options. Cost

	1 Feb 198	8 Feb 222	Rise 24p	12%
180	24	49	25	104%
200	13	32	19	146%
220	6	20	14	233%

Table 5.5 Gearing – rise over share price

of carry is important to large traders such as pension funds, unit trusts and market traders and unimportant to private investors.

The theory of options pricing suggests that option premiums are affected by interest rates in a second way. If interest rates are increased call premiums should also increase and put premiums decrease. Calls are looked upon as a delayed stock purchase, the money saved by buying calls can be placed on deposit to earn interest. Puts are looked upon as a delayed sale of stock that will result in the investor foregoing any interest that may have been earned from the sale of the stock.

However, in reality, an increase in interest rates will affect the underlying security market to a far greater degree, driving down the market with the result of call prices decreasing and put prices increasing.

	1 Feb 198	15 April 222	Rise 24p	12%
180	24	42	18	75%
200	13	22	9	69%
220	6	2	−4	−66%

Table 5.6 Gearing – rise over long period

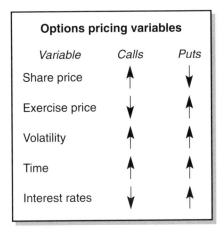

Figure 5.6 Movements in the variables and their effect on options premium

PRICING MODELS

The six variables we have just looked at are used together with a pricing model. Two of the best known are the 'Black-Scholes' and the 'Cox-Ross-Rubenstein' models. The prices generated by these models are known as *fair values* and are not necessarily what the options are trading at in the market (Fig. 5.5). The market price is derived from the fair value plus supply and demand, anticipation and the traders 'book'. However, armed with the fair value an investor can decide if an option is over or under priced and buy or sell accordingly.

THE GEARING EFFECT

The gearing effect of options is one element that makes traded options so attractive. It allows investors to, potentially, make very high profits for a minimal outlay on a relatively small movement in the underlying security price.

Table 5.5 shows that on 1 February the underlying security price is 198. One week later the share price has risen to 222, a rise of 24p or 12 per cent. If we look at the option's premiums the April 180 calls have risen from 24 to 49, a rise of 25 or 104 per cent. The 200 calls have risen from 13 to 32, a rise of 19 or 146 per cent and the 220 calls have risen from 6 to 20, a rise of 14 or 233 per cent.

In Table 5.6 the rise in the underlying security price is the same as in Table 5.5, but it has now taken place over a much longer period, almost three months. The options are now just about to expire. The Apr 180 calls have risen from 24 to 42, a rise of 18 or 75 per cent. The 200 calls have risen from 13 to 22, a rise of 9 or 69 per cent and the 220 calls have fallen from 6 to 2, a fall of 4 or 66 per cent.

The difference between the two examples is due to the erosion of time value in the second set of prices.

In Table 5.5 with the rise taking place over a short period there was no erosion or decay of time value in the option's premium. The lack of time value erosion, coupled with the increase in intrinsic value or the potential for acquiring intrinsic value, has resulted in the high percentage rise in all option premiums.

In Table 5.6 however, with the prices being taken just prior to expiry, the time value element of the premium has eroded to virtually zero. This leaves the premium made up almost entirely of intrinsic value.

Because of this it is important when buying options not just to get the direction of any price movement correct, but also the extent and the time scales involved. If a substantial rise or fall in the underlying security is expected over a short period, then out-of-the-money options will show the greatest increase. If the rise or fall is expected over a longer period then the in-the-money options should be purchased.

Movements in the variables

- If there is an increase in the share price the call premiums will increase and the put prices decrease
- An increase in exercise price will result in call prices decreasing and put prices increasing
- If volatility increases both call and put prices will increase
- The longer until expiry will result in increased call and put prices
- If interest rates are increased, because of the effect on the underlying security market, call prices will decrease and put prices will increase.

REVISION QUESTIONS – CHAPTER 5

1 There are five main variables used in calculating an option's premium.   T F

2 Intrinsic value is determined by the underlying security price and the exercise price.   T F

3 Time value is represented by that part of the premium not covered by intrinsic value.   T F

4 Time value increases the nearer an option is to expiry.   T F

5 Volatility measures a security's price movement over a given time period.   T F

6 Holders of call options are entitled to any dividends paid on the underlying security.   T F

7 The price produced by a pricing model is the market price of an option.   T F

8 If there is an increase in the underlying security price, call premiums will increase.   T F

9 An increase in volatility will result in a decrease in an option's premiums.   T F

10 The nearer an option is to expiry the faster time value will erode.   T F

11 The intrinsic value of an option is, for a call, the difference between the underlying security price and the exercise price, where the exercise price is below the current underlying security price.   T F

12 An option with intrinsic value is known as in-the-money. T F

13 With the underlying security price at 231 the 220 call option has no intrinsic value.   T F

14 A 330 put has 34p intrinsic value. The underlying security price is therefore 296.   T F

15 When intrinsic value is subtracted from an option's premium the amount left is known as time value.   T F

16 Work out intrinsic value and time value for the following prices.

	Share price 458	
Exercise price	Call	Put
420	39	3
460	12	18
480	2	30

17 Gearing allows investors to make considerable profits for a relatively small rise in the underlying security.   T F

18 If a sharp rise is expected in the underlying security in a short period, out-of-the-money options should be purchased.   T F

19 If the rise in the underlying security is over a long period, any increase in intrinsic value will be negated by the fall in time value.   T F

20 Due to the gearing effect it is not necessary to predict the time span of any rise or fall in the underlying security.   T F

6

STRATEGIES:
BUYING CALLS

In Chapter 3 we looked at the four basic trades of traded options. In the next four chapters we will look in more detail at when and why the four trades can and should be used.

BUYING CALLS

Call options are usually purchased in the expectation of the underlying security rising in value which will result in an increase in the value of the option. An investor may wish to use call options to take advantage of this rise for several reasons. The three most common being:

- *To gain exposure* to the price rise for a limited outlay and to use the options gearing to maximise profit
- *To maintain exposure* after the sale of a stock holding
- *To lock in a purchase price* while awaiting funds to acquire stock.

To gain exposure (speculative trade)

Many investors buy call options to gain exposure to an expected price rise in the underlying security. This strategy has the advantage, over buying shares, of the limited outlay required to gain control over a large amount of stock. In addition the gearing effect of options which allows for, potentially, a large profit for a relatively small movement in the underlying security is also very attractive.

An investor expects the shares of ABC Ltd to rise over the next few weeks. To participate in the price rise he purchases a call option.

The choice of which series to purchase depends on the investor's view of the extent and timing of the rise. The timing of the rise, or more correctly the time the rise takes, is possibly the most important factor in the choice of series. This is due to the possible erosion of the time value element of the option's premium.

If the rise is expected over a long period, in-the-money options should be purchased. In-the-money options have both intrinsic value and time value and will respond to any rise in the underlying security penny for penny. While the time value element of the premium will erode at an ever increasing rate, its percentage of the premium is considerably less than an out-of-the-money option where it is 100 per cent of the premium.

If the rise is expected to be over a short period, out-of-the-money options should be considered. The premium of out-of-the-money options comprises entirely of time value. As the underlying security price rises so the option moves towards acquiring intrinsic value at an ever increasing rate resulting in a high percentage increase in the premium.

Example 1

On 23 July ABC Ltd shares are 476 and the Aug 500 call has a premium of 4. By 11 Aug ABC Ltd shares are trading at 531 a 55p increase or 11.5 per cent. The Aug 500 call is now 33, a 29p increase or 725 per cent.

Once the option has increased in value and is trading at a profit, an investor may decide to *walk up* the position. This is a strategy that allows an investor to realise a profit and maintain an exposure to any future price rises in the underlying security.

Example 2

An investor anticipates a sharp rise in the underlying security and so purchases an out-of-the-money call option. The anticipated rise takes place forcing the option's premium to increase. The rise in the underlying security will lead to the introduction of new out-of-the-money series. The investor wishes to realise his profits but is concerned that the underlying security will continue to rise and does not wish to miss out on further increases in profits. By selling his options, which are now in-the-money and using some of the profits to purchase the new out-of-the-money options, the investor can realise his profits and maintain exposure to any continued price rises.

1 August	Purchase 10 Sep 500 calls @ 5
ABC Ltd 481	Cost of options £500
7 August	Sell 10 Sep 500 calls @ 22
ABC Ltd 515	Profit £2200–£500 = £1700
	Purchase 10 Sep 550 calls @ 2
	Cost £200
	Total profit £1500 + 10 Sep 550 calls

The strategy of walking up can be used to equal effect whether the investor is buying or selling calls or puts. As soon as an option has passed its usefulness it should be sold (bought back) and another option purchased (sold).

To maintain exposure

It is possible to maintain exposure to price movements in a stock after selling a holding. In this example an investor purchased 5000 shares in XYZ Plc at 126 as a long-term investment. The price has now risen to 158. The investor wishes to realise his profit, but is concerned that the price may continue to rise. By selling his holding at 158 the investor makes a profit of 32 per share (158–126). He can now use some of the profit to purchase 5 August 160 calls at 8. In so doing the investor has locked in a profit of 24 per share (158–126–8 = 24). And will still be able to participate in any future rise in the share price through the call option.

To lock in a purchase price

An investor expects the price of Mega Bucks Ltd to rise, but will not have sufficient funds available to purchase any stock for two months.

Not wishing to miss the opportunity the investor buys a call option. The option, giving the investor the right to buy the underlying security at the exercise price in the future, has secured the buying price of Mega Bucks Ltd for the investor. If the price of Mega Bucks Ltd does rise the investor can either exercise the option and purchase the shares or he can sell the option, realise his profit and purchase the stock in the market. By selling the option back into the market, the investor will receive the intrinsic value and any time value of the premium. If he had just exercised the option he would only realise the intrinsic value.

Example 3

The share price of Mega Bucks Ltd is 415. An investor buys one March 420 call at 24. The investor has locked in a purchase price of 444 (exercise price + premium) until March expiry. The share price of Mega Bucks Ltd rises to 456 and the premium of the March 420 call rises to 58. The investor can now purchase stock in one of two ways.

1 Exercise option and purchase stock at 444 (exercise price + premium).
2 Sell option at 58 and buy stock at 456 in the market. The investor has now effectively purchased stock at 422 [456– (58–24) = 422 (premium received – original premium)].

When purchasing the stock through exercising the option, the investor received only the intrinsic value. Selling the option back into the market, the investor receives both the intrinsic value and any time value in the premium. The only occasion that it would be ideal to exercise a call option early is immediately prior to a stock being declared ex-dividend. On being marked ex-dividend the underlying security will fall causing the call to drop in value. If the dividend is large enough the fall in the options premium may make it advantageous to exercise the option and acquire the dividend. However, the investor must ensure that the dividend is large enough to cover the original purchase price of the option and any commission charges. On all other occasions the option should be sold back into the market.

REVISION QUESTIONS – CHAPTER 6

1 Call buying can be used to gain exposure to a price rise in   T F
  the underlying security.

2 When buying calls to gain exposure an investor should   T F
  buy out-of-the-money series if the rise is to be over a long
  period.

3 When buying calls to maintain exposure to a stock after   T F
  selling a holding, the investor should use all of his profits
  to purchase the options.

4 The maximum loss when buying calls is unlimited.   T F

5 By exercising an in-the-money option, the holder only   T F
  receives the intrinsic value of the premium and not any
  time value remaining.

7

STRATEGIES: WRITING (SELLING) CALLS

Writing calls can reduce the risks associated with stock ownership and can make a portfolio less susceptible to volatile short-term market movements. Call writing can be aggressive or conservative depending on the series written and whether the position is covered or not.

Call writing falls into two categories, covered and uncovered (naked). The covered call writer holds stock, or purchases stock at the time of writing the option, to cover the position. This counters any threat of being exercised against, as the writer already holds stock that can be delivered to the holder. The uncovered call writer does not hold the stock and must therefore buy the underlying security in the market at the time of exercise. The market price of the stock will be considerably higher than the exercise price of the option, forcing the writer to trade at a loss. As the underlying security price continues to rise the uncovered writer is faced with the threat of an unlimited loss. Covered call writing is generally considered the more conservative approach to writing calls.

There are several reasons and scenarios for writing call options, the four main ones being:

- Enhancing the performance of an existing portfolio holding
- To offset the cost of stock purchase
- To secure a selling price and generate income
- To acquire downside protection in the event of a fall in the value of the stock.

PERFORMANCE ENHANCEMENT

The concept behind performance enhancement is to increase the earnings potential of a portfolio or an individual stock during periods of stable or falling prices. The premium received from writing options generates extra income, increasing the returns from a holding.

Example 1

An investor holds 5000 ABC Ltd shares bought at 130. The share price has now risen to 165 but is expected to fall slightly in the future. The extent of the expected fall does not warrant selling the holding or the purchase of puts. The investor decides to write call options. He writes a 5 Nov 160 call for a premium of 12. The option will not normally be exercised unless the underlying security price rises 160 the exercise price.

The underlying security price falls slightly as expected allowing the writer to keep the premium without the option being exercised. The returns on such a strategy can be expressed in one of two ways:

1 The return if the option is not exercised.

$$\frac{\text{Premium}}{\text{Net investment}} \times 100$$

$$\frac{12}{118} \times 100 = 10\%$$

This return is from the period that the strategy was in place for and can be annualised to show a return of 60 per cent.

2 The second way of expressing the returns offered by covered call writing is if the option is exercised.

$$\frac{\text{Premium} + \text{exercise price} - \text{original price}}{\text{Net investment}} \times 100$$

$$\frac{12 + (160-130)}{118} \times 100 = 35\%$$

Annualised this equals 212%.

A writer of call options should always know the returns from the position if the options are exercised or not. The selection of which series to write will be made easier with knowledge of the expected returns.

There will always be several different options series for the writer to sell. The choice of which one to use will depend on:

1 The expectations of the price movements over the life of the strategy. If the investor is neutral as to price movement then at-the-money options should be considered. At-the-money options will not usually be exercised, allowing the writer to keep the premium received. The premium of at-the-money options is made up entirely of time value which is at its greatest when the option is at-the-money. For a bullish expectation write out-of-the-money options. If the underlying security price does rise the option should not become in-the-money and remain unexercised. If the expectation is for a bearish movement in-the-money options should be written. The downward movement of the underlying security price will take the option from being in-the-money to at- or out-of-the-money and it will not be exercised.

2 The amount of return required will also determine which option is to be written. The higher the potential returns the higher the risk of being exercised against. Writing in-the-money options offers the greatest returns due to high premiums, but also carries the greatest risk of being exercised against and the stock being called away. The return from an out-of-the-money option will be less than an in-the-money option, but will carry far less risk of being exercised.

As the underlying security price moves it is possible to walk down all or part of the position (this is also known as rolling down). An investor has written an at-the-money call against an existing stock holding. The price of the underlying security falls as anticipated with the option moving to become out-of-the-money. The investor buys back the original at-the-money option at a profit and sells the new at-the-money options on the expectation of the underlying security either falling further or remaining stable.

BUY WRITE

A buy write strategy is used to reduce the cost of a stock purchase. The investor, while purchasing stock, writes a call option. The premium received from the sale of the option offsets the cost of the stock purchase.

Example 2

An investor wishes to purchase 5000 shares in XYZ Ltd as a long-term investment at 189. Simultaneously to reduce cost he sells a 5 Mar 200 call at 12. The premium received (12) has resulted in an effective purchase price of 177.

Buy 5000 XYZ Ltd at 189 = £9450
Sell 5 Mar 200 calls at 12 = £600
Net cost   £8850
Cost per share   177p

If the option is exercised, the investor must deliver stock at 200 (exercise price). However the investor has an effective purchasing price of 177 giving him a profit of 23 per share or 13 per cent.

SECURING A SELLING PRICE

It is possible to use a written call option to secure the sale price of the underlying security. Although puts are used to secure a sale price in a falling market, writing calls can secure the sale price in a rising market. The writer of the call also has the advantage of receiving the premium from the buyer, whereas the holder of a put must pay the premium.

Example 3

An investor holds stock at 415. If the stock reaches 460 it is considered overvalued and should be sold. The investor sells a Feb 460 call for 2. If the stock reaches 460 at or before expiry, the option will be exercised and the investor will have an effective selling price of 462 (exercise price + premium). If the underlying security does not reach 460 the option will not be exercised and the investor will keep the underlying security and the premium received as extra income.

DOWNSIDE PROTECTION

Option writing may be used to provide downside protection in the event of a slight fall in the market. The amount of downside protection is limited to the premium received and the amount of premium will depend on the series written.

Example 4

Mega Bucks Ltd is trading at 245 and the following calls exist:

Exercise price	May
220	32
240	15
260	6

Writing the May 220 calls (in-the-money) would give downside protection to 213 (underlying security price – premium 245–32 = 213). The 32 drop in the value of the underlying security would be offset by the premium received for writing the option. However if the underlying security price does not drop below 220 the chance of being exercised against is very high.

Writing the May 240 calls (at-the-money) would provide downside protection to 230 (245–15). Again, any drop in value of the underlying security will be offset by the premium received. The underlying security price now has to drop to 240 to avoid the possibility of being exercised against.

The May 260 calls (out-of-the-money) only provide protection down to 239 (245–6) but the likelihood of being exercised against is remote unless the stock rises to 260 (Fig. 7.1).

MARGIN

Writers of traded options are required to lodge margin with their broker. Margin acts as a form of insurance to ensure the writer has sufficient funds or the stock to deliver the underlying security if exercised against. The funds, in the form of cash, UK Gilts, US Treasury bills, German government bonds and certain UK equities are lodged with the broker for the duration of the position.

The minimum margin requirement is governed by the London Clearing House (LCH). Typically individual brokers set their own minimum requirements that are higher than those set by LCH. Margin requirements can and do change daily. By holding a higher minimum requirement than LCH stipulates, brokers are saved from the need of constantly demanding additional margin from writers as the market moves up and down.

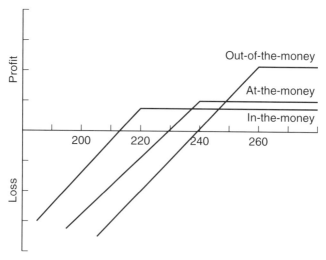

Figure 7.1 Downside protection

REVISION QUESTIONS – CHAPTER 7

1 Call writing falls into two categories, covered and uncovered.   T F

2 Uncovered or naked call writing is the safest form of writing calls.   T F

3 Writing calls can increase the returns from a portfolio.   T F

4 Call writing should be considered in stable or falling markets.   T F

5 A buy write strategy involves buying stock at the same time as writing the option.   T F

6 Writing calls cannot be used to secure a selling price of the underlying security.   T F

7 By writing a call option the writer receives downside protection by the amount of the premium received.   T F

8 Writers of calls are required to lodge margin with their brokers.   T F

9 Any type of security, including property, is acceptable as margin.   T F

10 Writing options is the most conservative strategy possible with options.   T F

8

STRATEGIES: BUYING PUTS

Puts, giving the holder the right to sell stock, are generally purchased in the expectation of a fall in the underlying security. This fall will result in an increase in the value of the put allowing it either to be exercised and the stock sold above the market price or traded back into the market for its premium at a profit.

Like calls, buying puts can be used for several reasons the most frequent ones being:

- To gain exposure to a fall in the price of the underlying security
- To hedge a position against an adverse price movement in the underlying security
- Lock in a sale price for future use.

TO GAIN EXPOSURE (SPECULATIVE TRADE)

The advantages of buying a put option are the same as those for buying a call. The premium paid out is the maximum loss a buyer can sustain and the gearing effect can result in high percentage profits for a relatively small price movement in the underlying security.

The choice about which series to purchase is yet another similarity with call options. Not only must the extent of the fall be anticipated but also the timing of the fall. If the fall is expected to be substantial and over a short period, out-of-the-money series should be purchased. If the fall is less substantial and over a longer period, in-the-money or longer dated puts are best.

It is possible, unlike calls, to purchase a long-dated put for little more than a short-dated put. This is due in part to puts being less popular than calls (supply and demand) and their profits being limited by the underlying security only being able to fall to zero. This situation can be an advantage if the underlying security does not fall at the speed the investor anticipates.

Example 1

It is 1 May and ABC Ltd is trading at 336. The expectation is that the share price will fall quite substantially over the next few weeks. To take advantage of this fall an investor purchases a June 300 put option at 3. Two weeks later the underlying security price has fallen to 317. The put premium has risen, to say 8. The investor can now sell the put option back into the market for a profit. While the option has not acquired any intrinsic value, the time value element of its premium has risen. This rise takes into account the fact that the option is now approaching being at-the-money where time value is greatest.

Once an investor is making a profit with a particular trade he may wish to walk down the position, realising a profit but maintaining his exposure to future price movements. To do this the investor must sell his options position back into the market, at a profit, while purchasing more options with a lower premium. By walking up his position the investor has recovered his initial investment, with a profit, and established a new position in a further out-of-the-money option at no cost. This new position can be looked upon as being risk free as it has cost the investor nothing.

Alternatively, if the investor believes the underlying security will not fall any further he can hold his in-the-money option and sell an out-of-the-money put option, thereby establishing a bear spread (spread trades are covered in depth later).

TO HEDGE AN EXISTING STOCK POSITION

Buying puts can be used to act as an insurance against a fall in the price of an individual security or, when using FT–SE 100 index options, the market in general. This strategy is known as a hedge and

Stock	Stock +/-	Option	Hedge +/-
310	−40	+33	−7
330	−20	+13	−7
350	0	−7	−7
370	+20	−17	+3
390	+40	−17	+23

Table 8.1 Hedged position

will result in any loss in the underlying security being offset by a rise in the value of the option position. While call writing will provide a limited amount of downside protection, only the purchase of puts can provide complete cover in the event of a substantial fall in the underlying security.

Example 2

An investor holds stock at 350 and anticipates a fall in its value. For tax reasons he does not wish to sell the stock and realise any profit. He decides to purchase a Dec 360 put at 17 to hedge his position. If the stock falls to 310, a fall of 40, the 360 put would have risen in value to offset this loss (Table 8.1).

The effect of the hedge has been, at the expiry of the option, to limit the loss of the investor to a maximum of 7. He is still able to participate in any rise although at a slightly reduced rate due to the premium paid out for the put option.

When establishing a hedge, it is necessary to determine the number of option contracts required. For a holding of 5000 shares five contracts would be required.

$$\frac{\text{Holding}}{\text{Contract size}} = \text{number of contracts} \quad \frac{5000}{1000} = 5$$

This is the simplest hedge available and depending on whether in- at- or out-the-money options are purchased, will depend on the actual performance of the hedge. In-the-money options will respond penny for penny with a fall in the underlying security. At-the-money options will generally move at half the rate of the underlying security and out-of-the-money options will respond the slowest to any price changes in the underlying security. The amount of protection will depend on how much an investor is willing to pay.

If the fall in the underlying security is expected to continue after the expiry of the hedge it should be rolled over into the next expiry month.

TO LOCK IN A SALE PRICE

Buying puts can also be employed to lock in the sale price of the underlying security. It is possible that due to an investor's tax situation he is not able to take advantage of high share prices and sell their holdings. By purchasing put options it is possible to lock in a sale price, to be used at a future date when an investor's tax situation may have changed.

REVISION QUESTIONS – CHAPTER 8

1 Puts are usually purchased in the expectation of a   T F
   rise in the underlying security.
2 Buying puts can hedge a position in the underlying   T F
   security against an adverse price movement.
3 If a large fall in the underlying security is expected over a   T F
   short period, out-of-the-money puts should be purchased.
4 Puts provide less downside protection than writing calls.   T F
5 If puts are used to hedge a position the investor cannot   T F
   participate in any future rises.

9

STRATEGIES: WRITING (SELLING) PUTS

Writing puts, like writing calls, fall into one of two categories, covered and uncovered (naked) writers. However in the case of puts, being a covered writer means the seller of the option has sufficient cash to purchase the underlying security if exercised against. The writing of put options can be used for two purposes:

- Generate additional income
- Lock in a purchase price.

GENERATE ADDITIONAL INCOME

Just as with call writing, selling puts can be used to generate additional income. The writer of a put receives the premium from the buyer. This premium represents the maximum profit the writer can make as long as the option remains unexercised at expiry.

The amount of additional income generated will depend on which series is written. An in-the-money series, with its high premium, will generate the highest returns but runs a far greater risk of being exercised. Out-of-the-money options, with their low premiums, will produce the least returns but are considered a much safer proposition against the threat of exercise.

As with all option writing strategies, margin is an important consideration. Investors must check with their broker about what they will accept as collateral and the amount required.

LOCK IN A PURCHASE PRICE

An investor takes a long-term optimistic view of a stock. However in the short term there is the possibility of a fall in its price due to, perhaps, unseasonal weather. The investor wishes to acquire stock at the lowest level possible and so writes a put option at the level he thinks the stock may fall to.

If the stock does fall below the exercise price the put will be exercised and the investor will be obliged to purchase the stock. The cost of the stock to the investor will be the exercise price minus the premium received, ensuring the investor purchases stock at the lowest level possible.

If the underlying security does not fall to the anticipated level the option will not be exercised. With the option unexercised the writer of the put will keep the premium received from the sale of the option as additional income.

REVISION QUESTIONS – CHAPTER 9

1 Being a covered put writer involves the seller holding the stock.   T F

2 Put writers do not have to submit margin.   T F

3 Writing puts can be used to lock in a buying price.   T F

4 The maximum profit for a put writer is limited to the premium received.   T F

5 A put writer is obligated to deliver stock if exercised against.   T F

10

ADVANCED STRATEGIES

While there are only four basic trades (buy call, sell call, buy put and sell put) it is possible to combine them in a number of different ways to achieve different risk reward profiles. The four basic trades are all open ended, that is they have either unlimited profit or loss potential. Combination trades are used to control risk and therefore most have limited profit and loss profiles.

SPREAD TRADES

The first types of combination trades we will look at are known as spreads. Spread trades are defined as the simultaneous opening purchase and sale of options within the same class (call or put) with the same underlying security. The options may have different exercise prices and/or expiry dates. One characteristic of spread trades is that maximum potential profit and loss is limited and therefore known in advance. Spreads can be classified into three types:

- Vertical
- Horizontal (calendar)
- Diagonal.

Vertical bull spread

A vertical bull spread involves the purchase and sale of calls with the same expiry date but with different exercise prices. The series purchased must have a lower exercise price than the one sold. This means the premium received from the sale of the higher exercise priced option will reduce the cost of purchasing the lower option. The result is a lower break-even point for the combined trade. The

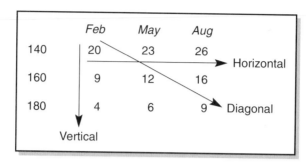

Figure 10.1 Spread classification

investor's expectation for such a trade is a small rise in the underlying security. In Fig. 10.2 he is expecting the underlying security to rise from 390 to 420 and is therefore willing to forego any upside participation of the 390 call above 420. This allows him to sell the 420 call, receiving the premium to offset the purchase of the 390 call.

Buy 1 Jan 390c at 16

Sell 1 Jan 420c at 7

Net debit   9

Maximum profit = spread – net debit.

$$420–390 = 30–9 = 21$$

Maximum profit is achieved if the underlying security price is at or above 420 at expiry.

Maximum loss = net debit of 9.

Breakeven = lower exercise price plus the net debit.

$$390 + 9 = 399$$

Advantages:

- The position can be established for less cost than a long call
- Breakeven is at a lower stock price
- Loss limited to net debit.

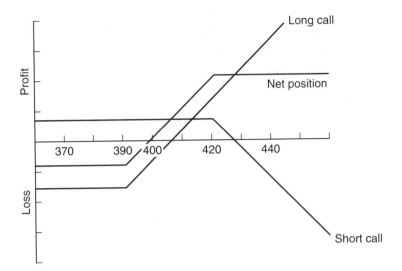

Figure 10.2   Vertical bull spread

Disadvantage:

● Profit is limited.

A bull spread is appropriate when a small rise in the underlying security is anticipated. Not only can bull spreads be constructed using calls but they can also be constructed using puts. Both calls and puts should be considered to determine which will provide the best risk/reward profile. When using puts the maximum profit and loss are calculated slightly differently. The position is established for a credit as the higher exercise-priced option, which is sold, will have the higher premium.

Maximum profit = Net credit.

Maximum loss = spread – net credit.

The break-even point = higher exercise price – net credit.

Vertical bear spread

If, instead of buying the lower exercise price and selling the higher exercise price, we reverse the situation and sell the lower and buy the

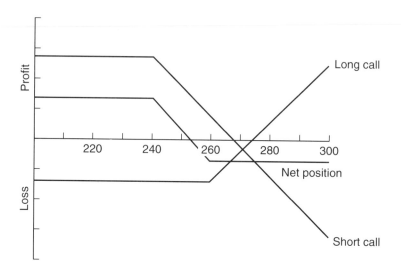

Figure 10.3 Vertical bear spread

higher exercise prices, we end up with a vertical bear spread (Fig.10.3). Vertical bear spreads should be considered if a slight fall in the underlying security is anticipated. In Chapter 7 we looked at selling calls in anticipation of a slight fall, however the position is margined and if the underlying security rises the writer is looking at, potentially, an unlimited loss. A vertical bear spread although still margined, is calculated at a lower rate helping the investor's cash flow. The overall position has a limited loss potential due to holding the higher exercise-priced option which, if the underlying security rises, will increase in value limiting the potential loss.

Sell 1 Jan 240c at   28

Buy 1 Jan 260c at 15

Net credit   13

Maximum profit = net credit of 13 and is achieved if the stock price at expiry is at or below the lower exercise price.

Maximum loss = spread – net credit.

$$260–240 = 20–13 = 7$$

Breakeven = lower exercise price plus the net credit.

$$240 + 13 = 253$$

Advantages:

- You receive net credit
- Limited loss.

Disadvantages:

- Limited profit
- Position will be margined
- Written option may be exercised early.

A vertical bear spread should be considered when a slight fall in the underlying security price is anticipated. Using a vertical bear spread allows an investor to reduce any risk should the expected fall in the underlying security not materialise. As with the vertical bull spread, bear spreads can also be constructed using puts, both should be looked at for their risk/reward profiles before choosing which one to use. The calculation of maximum profit and loss is also different. The position is established for a net debit as the higher exercise-priced option, with a higher premium, is purchased.

Maximum profit = spread − net debit.

Maximum loss = net debit.

Breakeven = higher exercise price − net debit.

Horizontal spread

Horizontal spreads are constructed by selling a near-dated option while at the same time buying a far-dated series with the same exercise price. The position or trade works due to the differences in the erosion of time value for options with different expiry dates. The erosion of time value, fastest when approaching expiry, works in favour of the writer of the near-dated option. With also being the holder of a far-dated option the difference between the prices of the two options will widen as the near-dated option approaches expiry.

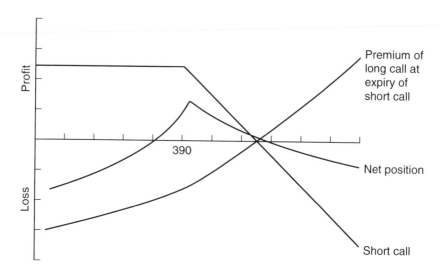

Figure 10.4 Horizontal or calendar spread

Once the near-dated option has expired, unexercised, the investor is left with a long position in the far-dated option at a reduced purchase price (Fig. 10.4). By using an at-the-money exercise price a neutral spread is constructed. An in-the-money exercise price will result in a bearish spread. If an out-of-the-money exercise price is used a bullish spread will be constructed.

Advantages:

- Limited loss
- Potentially unlimited profit.

Disadvantage:

- Written option may be exercised early.

A horizontal spread can be used if the investor expectation of the share price is neutral. This will allow the erosion of time value to take place with minimal possibility of the written call attracting intrinsic value and being exercised. Horizontal spreads should not be considered around the time of dividend payments as the written option may be exercised early, with no intrinsic value, for the dividend.

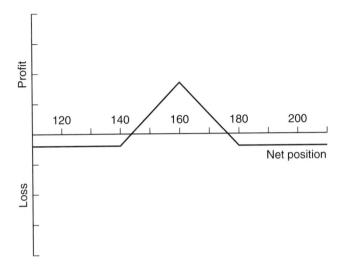

Figure 10.5 Butterfly spread

Diagonal spread

A diagonal spread entails the sale of a near month series with the pur-chase of a longer dated series with a higher exercise price. The investor's expectation is for a short-term fall in the underlying secu-rity price, allowing the near month written option to expire worthless, followed by a long-term rise when owning a long-dated option at a reduced price. The principle of time eroding at different rates, as in the horizontal spread, is again of prime importance.

Advantage:

• Unlimited profit potential.

Disadvantages:

• Early exercise of written series
• Position is margined.

Butterfly spread

By joining a vertical bull spread and a vertical bear spread together a butterfly spread can be created. A butterfly spread involves three exercise prices, with the same expiry date, equally spaced. One lower exercise price is purchased, two mid exercise priced options are sold and one higher exercise price is purchased. The ratio is always 1:2:1. The result is a trade with limited loss on both the up and down side and with maximum profit if the underlying security is at the mid exercise price at expiry (Fig. 10.5). It will be almost impossible to execute a butterfly spread as one trade and may involve the investor building the trade up over a period of time. This would be known in the market as *legging into*.

Buy 1 Dec 140c at 26

Sell 2 Dec 160c at 14

Buy 1 Dec 180c at 6

Net debit   4

Maximum profit = spread – net debit.

$$20-4 = 16$$

Maximum loss = net debit.

Breakeven:

Upside = higher exercise price – net debit.

$$180-4 = 176$$

Downside = lower exercise price + net debit.

$$140+4 = 144$$

A butterfly spread is appropriate for an investor who considers the underlying security will remain stable, but is not prepared to accept the unlimited risk associated with a short sale (selling calls or puts). Due to the number of contracts involved with a butterfly spread and the cost of commission and other charges, they are normally outside the financial resources of private investors.

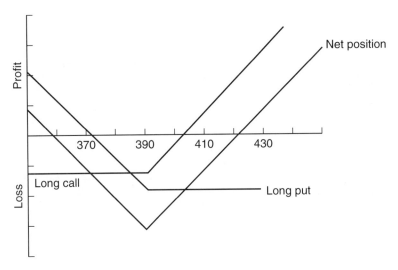

Figure 10.6 Long straddle

Straddle

A straddle involves the simultaneous purchase of the same number of calls and puts with the same exercise price and expiry date on the same underlying security (Fig. 10.6).

Buy 1 Sept 390c at 13

Buy 1 Sept 390p at 19

Net debit   32

Breakeven:

Upside = exercise price + net debit.

$$390+32 = 422$$

Downside = exercise price − net debit.

$$390-32 = 358$$

Maximum profit = unlimited.

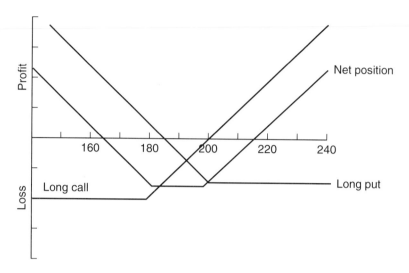

Figure 10.7 Long strangle

Advantages:

- Unlimited profit in either direction
- Loss limited to premium paid.

Disadvantage:

- Extended break-even points.

A straddle should be considered when the underlying security is at or near the exercise price to be used and the investor is expecting a dramatic move in prices but the direction is uncertain. If the underlying security falls the put option will increase in value, offsetting the loss (premium) on the long call. If the underlying security rises the call will rise in value offsetting any loss suffered on the put.

A straddle may also be considered when an increase in volatility is expected but direction is uncertain. The increase will result in an increase in the options premium without the price of the underlying security moving.

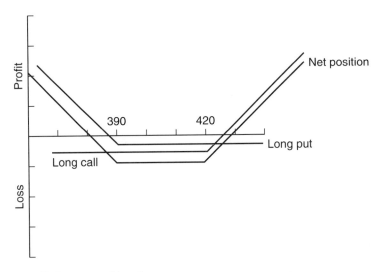

Figure 10.8 Long combination

Strangle and combination

The purchase of calls and puts with the same expiry date can be combined in a number of ways other than in a straddle. By purchasing calls and puts with different exercise prices a strangle or a combination can be constructed.

A long strangle involves the purchase of a call with a low exercise price and the purchase of a put with a higher exercise price; they are usually both in-the-money (Fig. 10.7). A long combination involves the purchase of out-of-the-money calls and puts, the call having the higher exercise price and the put the lower (Fig. 10.8). By using calls and puts with different exercise prices the investor has limited his maximum loss to a figure less than that with the straddle, however the maximum loss is extended over a larger price spread.

Strangle

Buy 1 Jan 180c at   21

Buy 1 Jan 200p at   15

Net debit   36

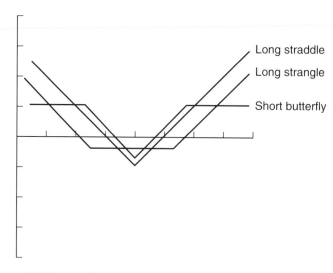

Figure 10.9 Risk reward comparison

Maximum profit = unlimited.

Maximum loss = net debit – intrinsic value.

Breakeven:

Upside = lower exercise price + net debit.

$$180+36 = 216$$

Downside = higher exercise price – net debit.

$$200-36 = 164$$

Combination

Buy 1 May 420c at 6

Buy 1 May 390p at 3

Net debit   9

Maximum profit = unlimited.

Maximum loss = net debit.

Breakeven:

Upside = higher exercise price + net debit.

$$420+9 = 429$$

Downside = lower exercise price – net debit.

$$390-9 = 381$$

A long strangle or combination should be considered if the underlying security is between the two exercise prices used and the market is stagnant. If the expected change in volatility does not materialise during the life of the strategy, the buyer of the strangle will be left with the intrinsic value of the two options as they are both in-the-money. With a combination, neither of the two options have intrinsic value as they are both out-of-the-money, which will result in the investor losing all the premium paid.

It is possible to compare the risk reward profiles for straddles, butterflys and strangles (Fig. 10.9). Straddles have the highest potential profit but also carry the highest risk of loss. Strangles offer a much smaller potential loss but over a greater price range. A short butterfly falls in between the two.

Ratio call spread

A ratio call spread entails the purchase of one call at a low exercise price and the sale of two or more calls at a higher exercise price, all with the same expiry date. The outcome will be a trade with limited loss on the downside (if the premiums are out of line this could result in a limited profit on the downside), a limited profit if the underlying security is at the higher exercise price but with unlimited loss potential on the upside (Fig. 10.10).

Buy 1 Nov 360c at 35

Sell 2 Nov 390c at 17

Net debit   1

Maximum profit = spread – net debit.

$$390-360 = 30-1 = 29$$

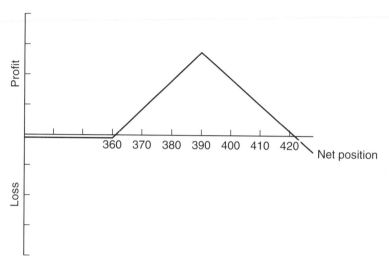

Figure 10.10 Ratio call spread

Maximum loss = unlimited.

Breakeven:

Upside = higher exercise price + spread.

$$390 + 30 = 420$$

Downside = higher exercise price + net debit.

$$360 + 1 = 361$$

The trade should be considered when the market is at or near the lower exercise price and the investor expects a slight rise in the market. The spread, while quite common, is seldom executed in a ration of more than 1:3.

Ratio put spread

The stablemate of the ratio call spread is the ratio put spread. It is constructed in a very similar manner to the ratio call spread. The difference being the sale of two or more options at the lower exercise price and the purchase of one option at the higher exercise price. The result is a trade that allows unlimited loss on the downside and lim-

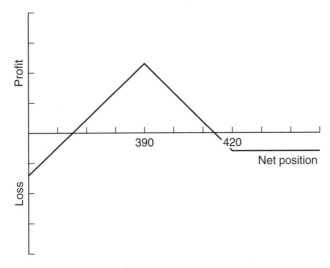

Figure 10.11 Ratio put spread

ited loss on the upside. Maximum profit is achieved if the underlying security price is at the lower exercise price at expiry (Fig. 10.11).

Sell 2 Apr 160 put at 5 = 10

Buy 1 Apr 180 put at   15

Net debit   5

Maximum profit = spread – net debit.

$$20-5 = 15$$

Maximum loss:

Upside = net debit = 5

Downside = unlimited.

Breakeven:

Upside = lower exercise + spread.

$$160+20 = 180$$

Downside = lower exercise – spread.

$$160-20 = 140$$

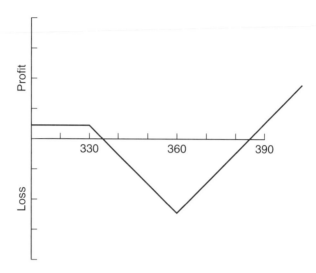

Figure 10.12 Ratio call backspread

A ratio put spread is appropriate when the underlying security price is at or near the higher exercise price and a slight fall is expected, although a sharp rise cannot be ruled out. Again ratio put spreads are not uncommon, but are rarely constructed at a ratio of more than 1:3.

Ratio call backspread

A ratio call backspread is the reverse of the ratio call spread where the number of calls purchased exceeds the number written. One call is written at the lower exercise price with two or more calls purchased at the higher exercise price. The result is a trade with limited loss on the downside and unlimited profit on the upside. Any loss is accepted if the underlying security is at or near the higher exercise price (Fig. 10.12).

Sell 1 May 330 call at   35

Buy 2 May 360 call at 15 = 30

Net credit   5

A ratio call backspread is usually considered when the underlying security price is near the higher exercise price and a rise is expected.

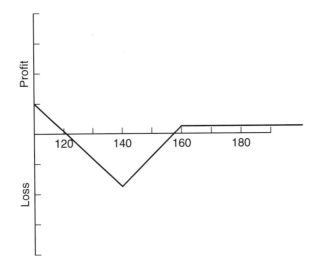

Figure 10.13 Ratio put backspread

Maximum profit = unlimited.

Maximum loss = spread – net credit.

$$30-5 = 25$$

Breakeven:

Upside = higher exercise price + maximum loss.

Downside = lower exercise price + net credit.

Ratio put backspread

The ratio put backspread is constructed by selling one put at the higher exercise price and buying two or more at a lower exercise price. The resultant trade has an unlimited profit potential on the downside and a limited profit on the upside. The maximum loss potential is when the underlying security price is at or near the lower exercise price (Fig. 10.13).

Buy 2 Nov 140 put at 3 = 6

Sell 1 Nov 160 put at   8

Net credit   2

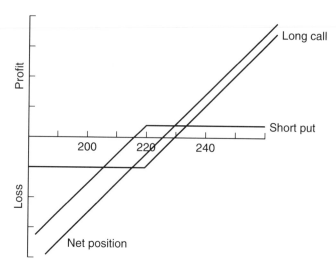

Figure 10.14 Synthetic long stock

Maximum profit:

Upside = net credit = 2

Downside = unlimited.

Maximum loss = spread – net credit.

$$20-2 = 18$$

Breakeven:

Upside = higher exercise price – net credit.

$$160-2 = 158$$

A ratio put backspread is normally entered into when the market is at or near the lower exercise price with the expectation of a fall in the underlying security price.

Synthetic long stock

By purchasing a call and selling a put with the same exercise price and expiry dates the result is a synthetic long stock position. The position has the same profit and loss profile as being long stock (Fig. 10.14). If the market rises the call option will gain in value and the premium from the short put contributes to the profit. If the stock falls the investor is looking at a potential unlimited loss, with the possibility of being exercised against with the short put.

Buy 1 Feb 220c at 10

Sell 1 Feb 220p at 4

Net debit 6

Maximum profit = unlimited.

Maximum loss = unlimited.

Breakeven = exercise price + net debit.

$$220+6 = 226$$

The long synthetic trade is a means of acquiring a position in traded options with the same profit and loss characteristics as a long position in the underlying security, but possibly at a reduced price.

Advantages:

- Unlimited profit on the upside
- Synthetically long position may be gained at a level below the current market price.

Disadvantages:

- Unlimited loss on downside
- The put may be in danger of early exercise.

Synthetic short stock

A synthetic short position involves the purchase of a put together with the sale of a call with the same exercise price and expiry date. The position established is equivalent to selling stock short (Fig. 10.15). The long put position gains in value as the underlying security falls in price; this is helped by the premium received from the sale of the call.

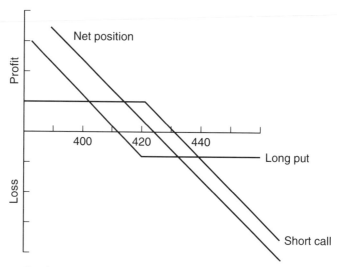

Figure 10.15 Synthetic short stock

If the underlying security rises, the 420 call will be exercised by the holder, forcing the writer to deliver stock at 423 (exercise price + net credit).

Buy 1 420p at   8

Sell 1 420c at   11

Net credit   3

As the position is a bearish one it may be used instead of selling the underlying security.

Advantage:

• Unlimited profit on the downside.

Disadvantages:

• Unlimited loss on upside
• Short call may be exercised early.

Conversion and reversion

The combination of a synthetic short position and the purchase of the underlying security produces a conversion. A conversion may be used either to create an arbitrage situation or to hedge a long stock position.

Buy 1 420p at   8

Sell 1 420c at   11

Net credit   3

Synthetic short stock = 423

If the underlying security can be purchased at less than the synthetic position (423) then an arbitrage situation exists. The investor has technically sold stock (synthetic position) and bought it back at a lower price, thereby locking in a profit.

If a synthetic long position is combined with the sale of the underlying security, a reversion is established. It is possible to create either an arbitrage situation or use the trade to hedge a short stock position.

Buy 1 Feb 220c at   10

Sell 1 Feb 220p at   4

Net debit   6

Synthetic long stock = 226

With the underlying security having been synthetically purchased at 226, if the investor can sell it above 226 then the investor will have locked in a profit.

REVISION QUESTIONS – CHAPTER 10

1 A spread trade limits both profit and loss.   T F
2 A vertical bull spread can be constructed with either   T F
   calls or puts.
3 The three exercise prices involved in a butterfly spread   T F
   must be the same amount apart.

4 A straddle involves the purchase of twice as many calls   T F
as puts.

5 A straddle and a combination will give the same profit   T F
and loss profile.

6 A condor trade involves four different exercise prices.   T F

7 To construct a ratio call spread an investor should buy   T F
one high exercise-priced option and sell two low-priced
options.

8 To construct a ratio put backspread an investor should   T F
buy one high exercise-priced option and sell two low-
priced options.

9 It is possible to construct an artificial stock position   T F
using options.

10 By combining a long synthetic stock position and selling   T F
the underlying security it is possible to create an
arbitrage situation.

11

RISK MANAGEMENT

The traded options market is designed for the management of risk, either by increasing or reducing exposure to it and can be used for this purpose by both private investor and professional alike.

The risk associated with buying shares can be broken down into two components, specific, and non-specific or market risk (Fig. 11.1). As the names suggest specific risk is associated with the stocks and shares of a specific company. It may be attributed to the company's product, market place or style of management. Market risk on the other hand affects the whole stock market and is more concerned with the economic outlook of the country and market sentiment.

It is possible to reduce specific risk to a minimum by holding a diversified portfolio. The more shares held, spread over a number of different sectors, will all but eliminate specific risk.

Market risk on the other hand cannot be diversified away. However, by using traded options market risk can be managed in an effective and efficient way.

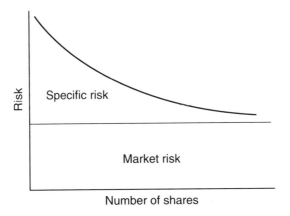

Figure 11.1 Specific and market risk

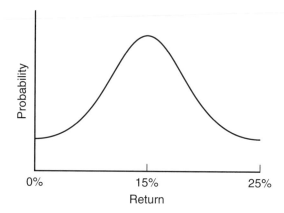

Figure 11.2 Risk reward for an individual share

The risk reward profile of an individual share or portfolio is illustrated in Fig. 11.2. It shows the expected return for the holding (15%), as well as the possibility of a very low return (0%) or a very high return (25%). The bell shape of a company's risk reward profile is known as a normal distribution curve and shows the probability of various returns at a number of different share prices.

By using traded options it is possible to manage and alter the risk reward profile to achieve a more desirable result.

HEDGING

Risk management in its simplest form involves the purchase of puts to act as a form of insurance against a possible fall in the market either in general or in an individual stock. This use of traded options is known as hedging and will result in an increase in the options premium to compensate for a fall in the value of the underlying security. This will result in modifying the left-hand tail or downside risk on the profile.

To design a simple hedge it is necessary to know the size of the contract to be used to establish the hedge and the amount of the underlying security to be hedged.

Example 1

An investor has a holding of 12,000 shares in ABC Ltd originally purchased at 325. He is concerned about the short-term economic news and wishes to protect the value of his holding. The share price now stands at 385. To calculate the hedge requirements proceed as follows:

$$\frac{\text{Number of shares to be hedged}}{\text{Contract size}} = \text{number of contracts}$$

$$\frac{12,000}{1000} = 12 \text{ contracts}$$

The options available are:

ABC Ltd 385

Exercise price	*Expiry date*		
	Jan	Apr	Jul
360	8	13	18
390	22	27	33
420	44	50	55

The investor decides to purchase the Jan 360 puts at 8. The cost of the hedge is:

Premium × number of contracts × contract size

8 × 12 × 1000 = £960

If the market falls, the value of the put should increase to compensate for the loss in value of the underlying security (Table 11.1).

Share price	Value of holding	Option P/L	Hedge P/L
335	40,200	+ 2040	42,240
345	41,400	+ 840	42,240
355	42,600	− 360	42,240
365	43,800	− 960	42,840
375	45,000	− 960	44,040
385	46,200	− 960	45,240
395	47,400	− 960	46,440
405	48,600	− 960	47,640
415	49,800	− 960	48,840

Table 11.1 Hedged position

While this simple hedge has prevented the value of the holding falling below £42,240 (Fig. 11.3) and therefore modified the left-hand or downside tail of the risk reward profile (Fig. 11.4) the hedge has not been completely successful in eliminating all the loss associated with a downward movement in the share price.

Although the hedge has not been completely successful it has ensured that the value of the holding does not fall below £42,240 or 352 per share, which means the investor has locked in a profit of 27p per share (Fig. 11.5).

The amount of profit locked in and the duration of the protection depends on which option series is purchased. If the July 420 option with a premium of 55 had been purchased the investor would have locked in a profit of 40p per share until the July expiry.

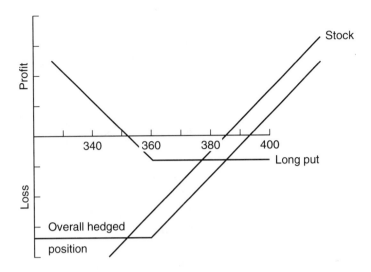

Figure 11.3 Hedged position

In order to establish a complete hedge it would be necessary to establish what is known as a delta neutral hedge. Deltas are dealt with in greater depth in Chapter 20, but for the time being an options delta is a mathematical value given to an option to describe the amount an options premium will change for a 1p change in the underlying security. It can also be thought of as the amount of underlying security to options contracts required to establish a neutral hedge. If an option has a delta of 0.5 its premium will change at half the rate of the underlying security, therefore twice as many option contracts will be required to cover or hedge the position. The calculation of a delta neutral hedge is as follows:

$$1/delta = number\ of\ contracts$$

Assuming the Jan 360 call option has a delta of 0.25 the number of contracts required to establish a delta neutral hedge will be:

$$1/0.25 = 4\ contracts$$

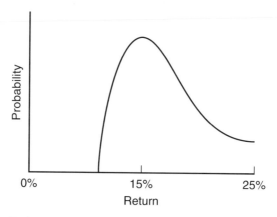

Figure 11.4 Risk reward profile with hedge

While a delta neutral hedge should move penny for penny with the underlying security, every time the underlying security changes so does the delta of an option. This movement in the delta will mean the investor no longer has a delta neutral hedge. Every time the delta of the option changes, the investor will either have to buy more options or sell some of those already held in order to maintain the position. This constant monitoring and adjustment makes delta neutral hedging time consuming and, potentially, very expensive on commission charges.

When designing a hedge for a portfolio it is necessary to use the FT–SE 100 index. The calculation for such a hedge is as follows:

$$\frac{\text{Value of portfolio}}{\text{FT–SE 100 index} \times £10}$$

An example of a hedge designed for a portfolio can be found in Chapter 4.

WRITING CALLS (PORTFOLIO ENHANCEMENT)

While buying puts will alter the downside risk of a risk reward profile, writing call options against an existing holding will sell off

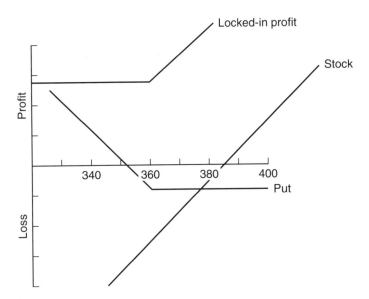

Figure 11.5   Locked-in profit

upside potential, due to the possibility of being exercised against, but will increase the probability of receiving the expected return due to the extra income generated by the options premium received.

The amount of additional income (premium) is governed by the investor's view of the stock, the required return, any downside protection required and the potential profit (covered in Chapter 7).

If the investor's view is neutral to price movements, at-the-money options would be appropriate due to the unlikelihood of them being exercised and their relatively high premium, made up entirely of time value. If the underlying security price is expected to rise slightly, out-of-the-money options should be considered. If the view is correct the underlying security price will rise, but the out-of-the-money option will not acquire intrinsic value, allowing the investor to keep both the premium received and the underlying security. With an expectation of a slight fall in the underlying security in-the-money options would be appropriate. The fall in the underlying security will result in the option losing intrinsic value and expiring out-of-the-money.

The amount of return will also have a bearing on which series is written. The highest returns are achieved with in-the-money options, but they tend to carry the largest risk of being exercised and the investor losing the underlying security. Out-of-the-money options offer the least returns but the risk of exercise and losing the underlying security are much reduced.

Writing call options can offer a small amount of downside protection. The amount of protection will depend on the series written and the amount of premium received (Chapter 7).

Example 2

It is 1 July and a fund manager has a portfolio of £1,000,000. He expects the market to fall or remain stable over the next two months and so decides to write call options to enhance the performance of the portfolio. The FT–SE 100 index stands at 3000. With a neutral view of the market the fund manager decides to write August at-the-money options (Aug 3000 call) for a premium of 74. The amount of options the fund manager can write is calculated as follows:

$$\frac{\text{Value of portfolio}}{\text{Contract size}} = \text{number of contracts}$$

$$\frac{£1,000,000}{30,000} = 33.3$$

The fund manager writes 33 Aug 3000 call options which will result in an additional income of £6600 (if this strategy had been used on an individual security the extra income generated would be in addition to any dividends paid during the life of the trade).

The returns from covered call writing can be expressed in two ways:

1 The return if the written call is not exercised.
2 The return if the written call is exercised.

Both of these returns can be shown for the duration of the strategy and as an annualised rate. The formulas for the returns are given in Chapter 10.

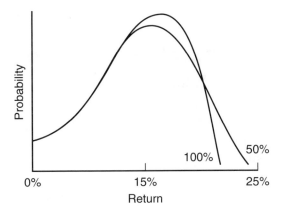

Figure 11.6 Writing covered call option

In Example 2 the fund manager wrote the full amount of option he could for the size of the portfolio. This would have resulted in a risk reward profile as depicted in Fig. 11.6. An alternative strategy would have been to write only a proportion of the amount of contracts available, e.g. 50 per cent or 16 contracts. This will result in a reduced additional income but if the neutral price expectancy was wrong any loss would be reduced (Fig. 11.6).

By combining buying puts and writing calls it is possible to alter both the left- and right-hand tails of the risk reward profile, while simultaneously increasing the probability of receiving the expected returns (Fig. 11.7).

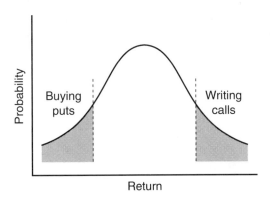

Figure 11.7 Modifying portfolio returns

REVISION QUESTIONS – CHAPTER 11

1 By holding a diversified portfolio specific risk can be   T F
  eliminated.
2 The risk reward profile is also known as the normal   T F
  distribution curve.
3 Purchasing call options will provide insurance in the   T F
  event of a fall in the value of the underlying security.
4 To calculate a simple hedge the formula is: T F
  number of shares to be hedged/exercise price.
5 A delta hedge has to be adjusted each time the underlying   T F
  security price changes.

12

TRADING AND SETTLEMENT

LONDON INTERNATIONAL FINANCIAL FUTURES AND OPTIONS MARKET

Traded options on UK equities are traded on the London International Financial Futures and Options Exchange (LIFFE). Its membership is made up of most of the world's leading banks and securities houses. The exchange operates a seat system; each seat, which entitles the holder to one market trader, is the equivalent of a company's share ownership. There are four types or classes of shares, each allowing the trading of a different range of products.

A Shares – Futures Membership

B Shares – Financial Options Membership

C Shares – Restrictive Membership

D Shares – Equity Options Membership

The trading on the market floor is regulated by exchange officials known as Pit Observers. Their role is to oversee trading to ensure compliance with the rules and regulations of the exchange. Their duties for the stock they are in charge of include:

- Ensuring an orderly market
- Calling trading halts
- Calling a fast market
- Monitoring attendance of market makers
- Accepting and trading Public Limit Orders.

Also on the market floor are the market makers and broker dealers. Market makers act as wholesalers buying and selling options on behalf of their firms. They are obliged to:

- Make a continuous two way price (bid and offer) in the stocks they are registered in
- Maintain a continuous presence on the market floor
- Ensure prices are regularly updated
- Trade in a specified minimum quantity.

In return for these undertakings market makers receive a reduced clearing fee on their trades. Market makers attempt to make a profit by buying cheap and selling dear.

Broker dealer is the term given to the stock brokers of the options market. They deal on behalf of private investors and fund managers not given direct access to the market. There are no laid-down rules or obligations for brokers but they must trade within the rules and regulations of the market. Broker dealers make their profit from commission charged and by dealing in options for their firm's account.

All traders on the market are qualified Registered Options Traders. To achieve this qualification the trader must pass a number of examinations in the theory of traded options and the workings of the market as well as serving an 'apprenticeship'.

TRADING

Trading is only allowed during official trading hours, 08.35–16.10 and is continuous throughout the day. At the start of business the exchange official will decide how to open the stocks he is responsible for. This may be by either an informal opening or by an opening rotation.

An informal opening will usually take place during periods of little or no interest in the options. Prices and trades may take place in any order and at numerous prices.

An opening rotation will be called by the exchange official if there is considerable interest and activity in the underlying security and option. The stock is opened series by series, starting with the near month calls. Once the calls have been rotated the exchange official will rotate the puts, again starting with the near month. Trades may only take place in the series being updated and only at one price.

Figure 12.1 Order route

Trading in options is conducted using the open outcry system. This means that all trades are transacted by market traders (market makers and brokers) face-to-face, on the market floor. All traders who are interested in the trade are entitled to hear all the information and participate if they wish. In order for this to happen the traders in a particular market sector (i.e. all chemical stocks) stand together in one area of the market floor. This area is known as a *pit* and the traders in the pit are known as a *crowd*.

When an investor passes his order to his broker (Fig. 12.1), it is checked before being passed on to the floor broker. The floor broker in turn will enter the appropriate crowd and ask for a quotation in the option series he is interested in. The market makers will quote their buying and selling prices (at this time they do not know if the broker is buying or selling). The floor broker will work out who is making the highest bid and the lowest offer prices before buying or selling as instructed by the investor.

When an option is deep out-of-the-money most investors abandon their options as worthless. However, some individuals and institutions need to quantify any losses for tax purposes. In order for this to happen a facility exists to sell a deep out-of-the-money option for a nominal price of 1p per contract. This is known as trading at *Cabinet* or *cab*.

PUBLIC LIMIT ORDER BOARD

Most orders from private investors are for execution at the market price (known as *at best*). While the investor is certain to deal, it may not be at the level he has decided is a fair price.

If an investor decides he wishes to trade at a particular price he can use the Public Limit Order Board (PLOB) if he cannot trade at this stipulated level straight away. The PLOB allows the investor's price to be displayed to the market, encouraging others to enter and deal at the stipulated price.

A Public Limit Order (PLO) is a firm dealing order and will be represented in the market until the end of the trading day or dealt or cancelled by the submitting broker. There is inevitably a delay in the broker receiving instructions to cancel the PLO and actually entering the market and cancelling the PLOB. If, during this time, the PLO is dealt the trade cannot be cancelled and will stand.

Example 1

The price spread in ABC Jan 390 call is 35 to 40.

The lower price of 35 is the price the market makers are prepared to buy at and is known as the *Bid*; 40 is the price the market makers will sell at and is known as the *Offer* or *Ask*. An investor decides the fair price for the Jan 390 call is 37 and is prepared to buy five contracts at that price. The cheapest price he can purchase the options at in the market is 40. The investor decides to enter his order on the PLOB. The new price spread will be 37 to 40.

The new 37 bid being the investor's PLO for five contracts. This increase in the Bid may well encourage a seller at that price. If the investor can purchase five contracts at 37 he will have saved 3.

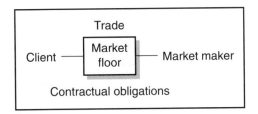

Figure 12.2 Contractual obligations

If the investor had purchased the options at 40 the Bid would have needed to increase to at least 41 for the investor to have made a profit (buy at 40 sell at 41). Having purchased the options at 37, the Bid only has to increase to 38 in order for the investor to make a profit using the PLOB (buy at 37, sell at 38).

In most cases PLOB trades, at their stipulated prices, are given priority over market makers trading at the same price. There are, unfortunately, a number of drawbacks with the PLOB. First, if the investor wishes to purchase five contracts but the seller only wishes to sell one, the investor must buy the one contract. He must then wait and see if he can buy the remaining contracts at a later time during the trading day. Apart from the price no conditions can be attached to the PLO. The second drawback is that the investor may find himself chasing to price up or down. If, as in the example, the price spread is 35 to 40 the investor goes on the Board at 37 and changes the spread to 37 to 40. The underlying security price rises, pushing the options premium up to 38 to 42. The investor's PLO will not be fulfilled at 37 and he has lost the opportunity to buy the options at 40. He must now either submit a new PLO at, possibly, 39, buy his five contracts at 42 or walk away from the trade.

The Public Limit Order Board is extremely under-utilised on LIFFE. Less than 1 per cent of business in the UK is conducted using the PLOB, compared with approximately 25 per cent of business on the European Options Exchange in Amsterdam.

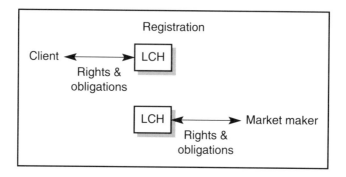

Figure 12.3 Rights and obligations

SETTLEMENT

Both parties to the trade, the broker and the market maker, will enter the details on a dealing slip or card. The slip is in turn handed to members of the exchange who enter the details into a computerised matching system to ensure both parties have exactly the same details. As this is happening the trade may be reported back to the investor for his information. Once the trade has been matched, the details are passed onto the London Clearing House (LCH) for registration.

When a trade has taken place and matched there is a contractual obligation between the two parties (Fig. 12.2). Once the trade is registered with LCH all links between the two trading parties are broken and any rights or obligations are between the investor and LCH (Fig. 12.3). This system means that LCH is the guarantor for all trades on LIFFE and no one is at risk from counter-party credit ratings.

Payment for any options trade must be made to LCH by 10.00a.m. the following business day. However most brokers will demand payment (including commissions) at the same time as accepting the order and trading.

At 16.10 the closing procedure will start. As with the opening procedure the exchange can close the stocks in his charge by either an informal closing or a closing rotation depending on the amount of interest and on price movements in the underlying security. Trading may continue in busier stocks as the prices are updated before being closed.

EXERCISE PROCEDURE

If a holder of an option wishes to exercise his rights and buy (call) or sell (put) the underlying security, he must instruct his broker to enter an exercise notice to LCH, on his behalf. With the link between the buyer and seller having been broken, upon the submission of an exercise notice, LCH randomly assigns a broker with an investor who has written an option identical to the one being exercised to either deliver or take delivery of the underlying security.

The computerised random selection process takes place overnight once all the day's trades have been processed. This allows writers to close out their positions, during trading hours, without fear of being exercised against that evening.

The selection by LCH will not identify an individual writer of an option, but a broker with at least one investor who has written an option identical to the one being exercised. The broker must then, again by random computerised selection, identify and notify the writer.

Once the option has been exercised the details of the equity trade are entered into the London Stock Exchange's settlement system by the two brokers concerned. This is then matched as a standard share purchase and sale and settled on the appropriate Stock Exchange account day. Equity options may be exercised on any business day, except the last day of a Stock Exchange account period, and at any time until 17.20.

American style index options may be exercised on any business day until 16.31. European style index options may only be exercised on their expiry day until 18.00. On all expiry dates exercise times are extended to 18.00 to take into account the extra amount of exercise instructions received by LCH.

REVISION QUESTIONS – CHAPTER 12

1 The official trading hours for LIFFE equity options are 08.35–16.30.　　T F

2 Trading is conducted by open outcry by market traders on the market floor.　　T F

3 The market is regulated by Pit Observers on the market floor.　　T F

4 Once a trade has been transacted, it is checked before being registered with LCH.　　T F

5 Payment for purchased options must be with LCH by 09.45.　　T F

6 Once a trade is registered with LCH, any link between the trading parties is broken.　　T F

7 After exercise notices have been submitted, LCH assigns a writer on a 'first in, first out' basis.　　T F

8 Equity options may be exercised on any business day, except the last day of a Stock Exchange account period.　　T F

9 The latest an equity option may be exercised is 18.00.　　T F

10 The latest time for exercising an American style option is 16.31.　　T F

11 The Public Limit Order Board reduces an investor's exposure to the price spread.　　T F

12 The PLO is not a firm dealing order and must be confirmed with the investor before being dealt.　　T F

13 The submitting broker can make the PLO conditional on the whole order being filled.　　T F

14 PLOs can only be withdrawn at the end of the day's trading.　　T F

15 Most of the private investor business on LIFFE is conducted through the PLOB.　　T F

13

CHOOSING A BROKER

All investors wishing to trade in traded options must deal through a broker who is qualified to trade on LIFFE. There are a number of brokers willing to accept private client business, but all offer slightly different services and charges. When it comes to choosing a broker it is important to ensure that you know, not only what services there are to choose from, but also your own requirements.

The services and the quality of the services differ greatly from one firm to another. When approaching a broker for the first time it can be an advantage to write down a list of questions to ask. Some of the questions you may want the answers to are as follows.

What regulatory body does he belong to? There are a number of different regulatory bodies, exchanges and associations that brokers can belong to. They must be members of the Securities and Futures Authority (SFA). The SFA is a self regulatory organisation (SRO) under the 1986 Financial Services Act, established to regulate business, including dealing and arranging deals, in all types of securities and in futures and options. In addition to being members of the SFA, brokers may be members of an exchange, if not they must deal through a second party who is an exhange member. Finally, there is the Association of Private Client Investment Managers and Stockbrokers (APCIMS). APCIMS is best described as a trade association representing the interests of private client stockbrokers and, through them, the private investor. The first questions must be: are you a member of the SFA? to what exchanges do you belong? and are you a member of APCIMS?

Under the SFA and the exchanges concerned a number of professional exams and qualifications have been established. They range from the Registered Options Traders (ROT) exam, which allows brokers to transact business in equity traded options to the Registered

Representative exam, allowing a person to give independent financial advice on futures and options. What qualification does the person you will be dealing with have? Is he/she an ROT and/or a registered representative? Some firms who offer an execution service only and give no advice may not require such qualifications, if not what experience and knowledge does your contact have?

The prices on the traded options market rarely stand still for long, how long will the broker take to transact your business once you have given him the details and will it be confirmed back to you or not?

Is there any minimum account balance you are required to maintain, if so how much and for how long? What is the minimum deal the broker will consider (one contract or ten)?

Does the broker publish a newsletter on traded options. How often is it published and how is it distributed? (It's no good the broker making recommendations if they are out of date by the time you receive them.)

Finally, ask friends and colleagues if they have any recommendations. Their experiences may well give good indications of firms to be approached or avoided.

Different brokers charge different rates of commission and contract charges for the same service. Investors must be prepared to shop around and negotiate with brokers to achieve the best deal. Being charged too much can be the difference between making a profit and making a loss. Example 1 shows two sets of typical charges for buying five call options for a premium of 23p and selling at a premium of 32p.

Example 1

Broker A

Purchase

Premium	(23p × 1000 × 5)	1150
Commission	1.5% or £20 min	20
Contract charge	£1.50/contract	7.5
		1177.5

Sale
Premium	(32p × 1000 × 5)	1600
Commission	Half comm. on closing	−10
Contract charge		−7.5
		1582.5

Purchase	1177.5
Sale	1582.5

Net profit	405

Broker B

Purchase
Premium	(23p × 1000 × 5)	1150
Commission	2.5% or £30 min	30
Contract charge	£2/contract	10
		1190

Sale
Premium	(32p × 1000 × 5)	1600
Commission	2.5% or £30 min	−30
Contract charge	£2/contract	−10
		1560

Purchase	1190
Sale	1560

Net profit	370

The number of contracts purchased, the commission and contract fee charged will affect the profits. If only one contract is purchased with commission of £20 and contract fee of £1.5, the options premium will have to rise by 2.5p to 25.5 just to cover the charges. However if five contracts are purchased with the same charges, the options premium will only have to rise by an extra 0.5p to 26 to cover the additional contracts.

Once you have all the information from a number of brokers a decision will have to be made on the type of service you require and the charges you are prepared to pay. The services on offer from brokers fall into one of three categories:

Discretionary. With this type of service the investor leaves all investment decisions to the broker and will not normally be consulted. This service is for those investors with a considerable amount of money to invest but with little or no time and/or inclination to conduct their own investments.

Advisory. An advisory service is for investors who wish to maintain control over their investments but do not want to conduct their own research. They will receive advice and recommendations from their broker but the final decision is theirs.

Execution only. With this service the investor receives no help from the broker. He must conduct his own research and must make his own decisions. The broker will only execute the investor's orders in the market for him.

The type of service best suited to an individual investor will depend on:

- The amount the investor is prepared to pay
- The level of knowledge and sophistication of the investor
- The amount of time and effort that the investor is prepared to spend on research and stock selection.

Once a decision and contact has been made with a broker, the appropriate forms (together with a cheque or another form of payment) will have to be completed and returned to the chosen broker. Amongst the forms will be a risk warning letter to be signed and returned. While this sounds ominous it is just to say that the investor understands the risks associated with traded options. The letter is a hang up from when options were first introduced to the UK and were perceived to be a high risk investment.

When confirmation of the account is received dealing can commence. Instructions for most deals will be given over the telephone, so it is important to ensure that the correct information is given clearly and concisely. A suggested format is:

1 Buy/Sell.
2 Quantity.
3 Underlying security.
4 Expiry month.
5 Exercise price.
6 Call/Put.
7 Open/close.
8 Premium/at best.

Example 2

'I wish to:
　Buy
　5
　Sainsbury
　November
　420
　Calls
　To open
　at 14'

It is recommended that before any deals are undertaken for real a number of ghost trades are entered into. Ghost trading is a method of testing the market and any theories before committing any money. Details of proposed trades are written down, together with the reasons behind the trade, expected price movements and the eventual outcome. It is then possible to see if the trade would have behaved in the expected manner and the theory of traded options are thoroughly understood. It is important to be particularly honest in ghost trading, if the stock moves in the anticipated direction but for the wrong reason then the reasons for undertaking the trade are not valid. The more success when ghost trading is undertaken, the greater the chances of successful trading in the future.

And last, but by no means least, if you do not understand anything, ask your broker for an explanation. You, the investor, are in charge and if you are not happy either say so or go elsewhere.

REVISION QUESTIONS – CHAPTER 13

1 Brokers are not required to belong to any regulatory body.   T F
2 In order to trade on the options market floor a broker must   T F
   have passed an exam.
3 Contract charges differ from broker to broker.   T F
4 The cheapest service offered by brokers is a discretionary   T F
   service.
5 If ghost trading is used a broker still requires payment   T F
   of commission charges.

14

CHOOSING A STOCK

When choosing which underlying security to buy options on, it is important to predict not only the direction of any price movement, but also the extent of the movement and the time scale involved. One of the best methods of determining these requirements is by *Technical Analysis*.

Technical Analysis is the study of supply and demand and involves plotting and studying price and volume data on charts. Technical Analysts believe prices move in repeating and recognisable patterns known as trends. Using these trends, buy and sell signals are identified. There are many different and varied areas to TA that may be used in isolation or in conjunction with each other. It is up to the individual to decide which areas to use and which to leave alone.

CHARTING

To show the patterns and trends of price movements they are plotted on charts. There are three types of charts that can be used:

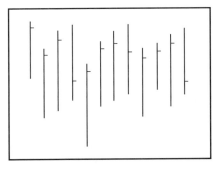

Figure 14.1 Bar chart using high, low and closing prices

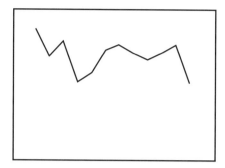

Figure 14.2 Line chart using closing prices

- Bar chart
- Line chart
- Point and figure chart.

Bar charts. Bar charts involve plotting the period's high and low prices connected by a line (Fig. 14.1). The closing price for the period is then plotted as a small horizontal line.

Line charts. Line charts are the simplest charts to construct using only the closing price for the period, as some TAs believe that the closing price is the most important (Fig. 14.2).

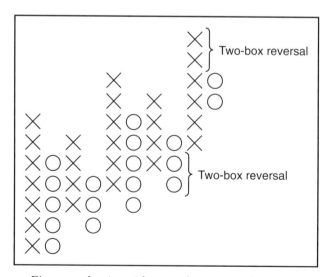

Figure 14.3 Figure and point with a two-box reversal

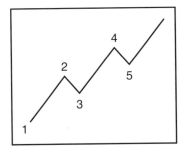

Figure 14.4 Rising tops

Point and figure charts. Point and figure charts do not take time into consideration, they are only a study of price movement (Fig. 14.3). As the price rises an 'X' is plotted forming a vertical column. When the price suffers a reversal an 'O' is plotted in the next column. This is continued as long as the price continues to fall. When the price rises a new column of 'X's is formed. Usually the price has to reverse by a specified number of boxes before a new column is started.

TRENDS AND PATTERNS

Trends and patterns form within charts and may be up, down or sideways, but sooner or later they will change. The sooner a trend is recognised the easier it is to follow, allowing early detection of changes and reversals which offer profit potential. The four basic trends and patterns are:

Rising tops. Rising tops occur in a rising market as prices reach progressively higher and higher tops interrupted by a slight pause for breath. The share price starts at 1 (Fig. 14.4) and rises as buyers outnumber sellers, driving the price up to 2. At 2 the previous buyers start taking profits and the price slips back to 3. However, the overall upturn in the value of the shares attracts more buyers who again outnumber sellers forcing the price to rise to 4. The process continues with each high being higher than the previous high.

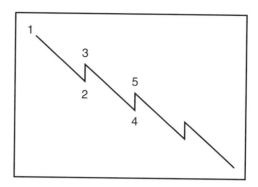

Figure 14.5 Falling bottoms

Falling bottoms. Falling bottoms form during a fall in the market with successfully lower bottoms. The share price starts at 1 (Fig. 14.5). With sellers outnumbering buyers the price falls to 2, where buyers enter the market forcing the price up to 3. At 3 the buyers start taking profits which will bring more sellers than buyers into the market forcing the price down to 4. Once the price hits 4 more buyers again enter the market looking for a quick profit, forcing the price back up to 5. The process continues until more buyers enter the market on a long-term basis forcing the trend to reverse.

Support levels. The support level of a stock is a price level at which the stock price receives support preventing the share price from falling further. In Fig. 14.4, 3 and 5 were support levels and in Fig. 14.5, 2 and 4 are support levels. In general, support levels occur when there is sufficient demand for the shares at a particular level forcing the price higher (Fig. 14.6).

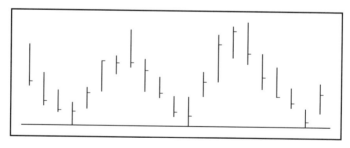

Figure 14.6 Support levels

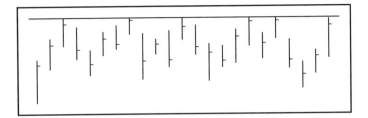

Figure 14.7 Resistance levels

Resistance levels. The resistance level of a stock is formed when supply outweighs demand forcing the share price to decline. In Fig. 14.4 resistance levels were found at 2 and 4. In Fig. 14.5, 3 and 5 are resistance levels. As with support levels resistance levels can be both short and long term (Fig.14.7).

It is not unusual that once a share price has broken its resistance level it will then become a new support level (Fig. 14.8).

PATTERNS

Once a trend has been established it will continue until a major reversal occurs. Some reversals are relatively short and are not easy to pick up whereas major reversals take a greater time to develop, giving a more reliable signal. Some signals or patterns happen on a frequent basis, whereas others only occur infrequently. The five patterns concentrated on here are quite common and are easy to identify. They are:

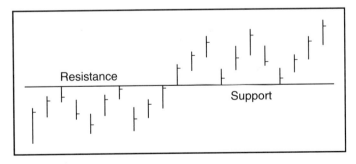

Figure 14.8 Change in resistance to support

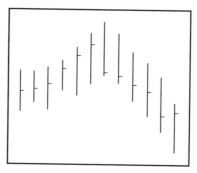

Figure 14.9 Key reversal (top)

- Key reversals
- Head and shoulders
- Triangles
- Rectangles
- Wedges.

All patterns occur both at the top and bottom of trends.

Key reversals

Key reversals usually occur in thinly traded stocks after a period of unusually high activity which was preceded by a long unbroken rising

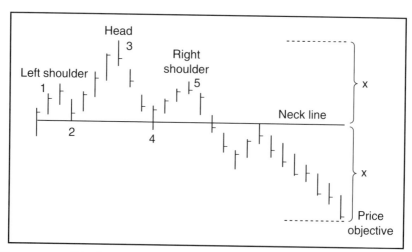

Figure 14.10 Head and shoulders (top)

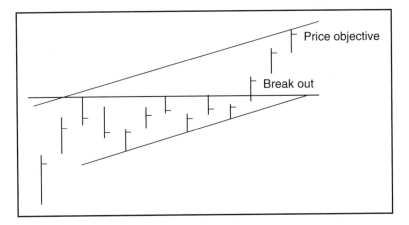

Figure 14.11 Ascending triangle

or falling trend (Fig. 14.9). The reversal will usually occur in a single day or trading session. Key reversals are quite common and may become part of a larger pattern.

Head and shoulders

Head and shoulders (Fig. 14.10), form when prices rise to a high 1 (left shoulder) before falling back to a low at 2 (this is the start of the

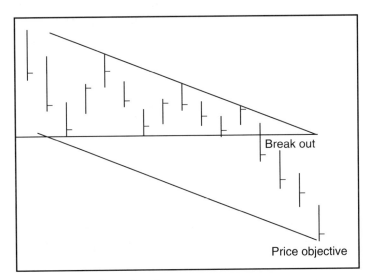

Figure 14.12 Descending triangle

neck line). At 2 buyers again outnumber sellers forcing the price to a high 3, the head. The new high must be higher than the previous high at 1. The price again falls from the new high back to the neck line at 4. The neck line acts as a support level and the buyers return forcing the price to rise to 5. This new high is lower than the head and forms the right shoulder. As the price falls from the right shoulder it breaks the neck line before recovering slightly. The price objective is the same distance from the neck line as the head is above it.

Triangles

Triangles can be either ascending or descending. Ascending triangles are formed by a horizontal resistance line with an upward sloping support line. Ascending triangles (Fig. 14.11) give an indication of a bullish future, while descending triangles (Fig. 14.12) offer a bearish outlook.

For an ascending triangle each time the share price reaches the resistance line supply overtakes demand and the price falls back to the support line. At the support line buyers enter the market forcing prices up to the resistance line again. Each time this happens the support is found at an increasingly higher level narrowing the trading price range. Once break out, through the resistance line, is achieved the price objective is measured by a line drawn parallel to the lower support line starting from the top that first touched the resistance line.

Rectangles

A rectangle is formed when a share continually trades within the boundaries set by horizontal support and resistance lines. Each time the share price reaches the resistance line supply outstrips demand forcing the price lower (Fig. 14.13). When the share price reaches the support line, more buyers than sellers are in the market forcing the price higher. The price objective after break out is the height of the rectangle above the resistance line or below the support line. Once a rectangle has developed it offers an excellent opportunity for short-term trading, buying when the share price is at or near the support line and selling when it is at or near the resistance line.

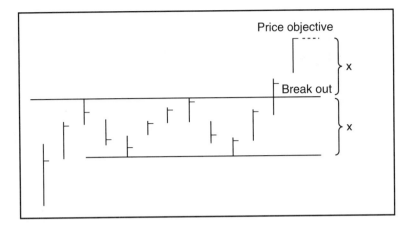

Figure 14.13 Rectangle

Wedges

Wedges are formed when the share price trades between two converging support and resistance lines in the same manner as a triangle. However in a wedge pattern the support and resistance lines are inclined either up or down. An upward sloping wedge is known as a rising wedge (Fig. 14.14), with a downward sloping wedge being known as a falling wedge.

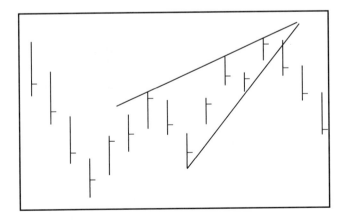

Figure 14.14 Rising wedge

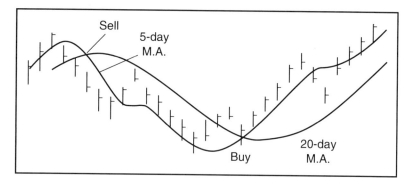

Figure 14.15 5-day and 20-day moving averages

The vast majority of trends and patterns can be formed during major (primary) or secondary trends. A primary trend can last for several years before reversing. Within each primary trend will be a secondary trend lasting a number of months before it is reversed. Inside each secondary trend it is possible to identify short-term trends. While short-term trends may only last a number of weeks and therefore do not offer the opportunity for long-term investment, if identified early enough they offer an excellent opportunity for short-term trading and profit.

MOVING AVERAGES

Moving averages indicate an underlying trend. They show the average of a share price over any given time period. A five-day moving average is the average of the last five days' share prices. When share prices are rising, moving averages will also be rising although, depending on the days used, the moving average will lag behind the actual share price.

If two or more moving averages are plotted together, one short term (say five day) and one longer term (say 20 day), crossovers will occur between the two as the share prices reverse. These crossovers can be used as buy and sell signals. When the five-day ascending (or rising) moving average crosses the descending (or falling) 20-day moving average (Fig. 14.15) a buy signal is generated. Should the five-day average be falling when it crosses the rising 20-day average a sell signal is produced.

Moving averages can also be used as stop loss levels. If, for example, the share price moves below the five-day moving average the stock or the option should be sold.

RELATIVE STRENGTH INDEX (RSI)

The RSI measures the rate at which prices move. In theory, it ranges from 0 to 100 but in practice the range is from 10 to 90.

The RSI is calculated over a given period of, for example, 15 days. Normally an RSI over 80 is considered overbought while an RSI below 20 is considered oversold.

RSI is more effective in detecting divergence and convergence. A divergence occurs when share prices attain a series of highs while the RSI shows low peaks. This is considered a sell indicator.

Convergence occurs when share prices produce a series of low prices while the RSI shows higher levels. This situation can be considered a buy signal.

FUNDAMENTAL ANALYSIS

An alternative approach to choosing a stock is fundamental analysis. Fundamentals use management accounts to produce ratios and percentages. The aim of these ratios and percentages is to show if a stock is under or over valued and worth buying or selling. Fundamental analysis however will not show how far a stock is likely to move or in what time scale.

EARNINGS PER SHARE

The earnings per share ratio will show the amount of profit (loss) each share has earned after losses and extraordinary items have been taken into account. The earnings per share is calculated as follows:

$$\frac{\text{profit attributed to share holders}}{\text{number of shares in issue (ranked for dividends)}}$$

PRICE/EARNINGS RATIO

The price/earnings ratio will show the number of years at the present earnings needed to cover the current market price. The price/earnings ratio is calculated as follows:

$$\frac{\text{current market price per share}}{\text{earnings per share}}$$

P/E ratios need to be judged in relation to other stocks in the same market sector. A stock with a high P/E ratio, when compared to the sector average, would imply a stock in demand, whereas a stock with a low P/E ratio suggests a company with poor growth prospects. P/E ratios are readily available in the city pages of all quality newspapers.

EARNINGS YIELD

The earning yield expresses the earnings per share as a percentage of the current market price. To avoid confusion with dividend yield the earning per share is grossed up. Earnings yield is calculated as follows:

$$\frac{\text{earnings per share} \times 100/75}{\text{current market price}} \times 100$$

DIVIDEND YIELD

In order to compare net dividends to other investments that are paid gross, such as bank deposits and gilts, the dividend needs to be grossed up. A company with a high dividend yield is not regarded as a high growth prospect, whereas a company with a low dividend yield is considered to have high growth potential. Dividend yield is calculated as follows:

$$\frac{\text{gross dividend per share}}{\text{current market price}} \times 100$$

Companies with a high P/E ratio tend to have a low dividend yield and companies with a low P/E ratio tend to have a high dividend yield.

DIVIDEND COVER

The dividend cover of a company will help an investor decide if present dividends are likely to be maintained, increased or decreased in the future. Dividend cover is calculated as follows:

$$\frac{\text{earnings per share}}{\text{net dividend per share}}$$

If a company has a high dividend cover it is not distributing all the profits it could to the share holders. This may indicate a cash surplus is being built up in readiness for an acquisition, but it can also make the company an attractive takeover target. A company does not have to have adequate cover to pay a dividend but can pay the share holders out of reserves.

NET ASSET VALUE

The net asset value of a company is its tangible or intrinsic value. The net asset figure used in the calculation is taken from the company accounts and is therefore an historic figure and may not portray the real or present value of the assets. Net asset value is calculated as follows:

$$\frac{\text{net assets}}{\text{number of shares in issue}}$$

Net asset value can be of particular interest during a takeover.

UK ECONOMIC FIGURES

When choosing which traded options to buy or sell it is not enough just to analyse the performance potential of the underlying security; an investor must understand what is happening in the economy. The following give a brief description of the main UK economic figures.

Retail price index (RPI)

The RPI shows increases and decreases in inflation and is published monthly by the government. The index comprises a basket of services and goods, with their prices taken at a number of different places around the country by the Family Expenditure Survey. It is the changes in the index which are used when inflation is quoted.

Balance of payments

The balance of payments shows the total value of goods and services imported and exported which is now calculated by VAT returns. A surplus in balance of payments means the country is earning money from the companies and countries buying our goods and services.

A deficit in the balance of payments means the country is spending money which has to be paid for either from the government's foreign reserves or from borrowing abroad, both of which have an inflationary effect on the economy.

Public Sector Borrowing Requirement (PSBR)

A government running a deficit, i.e. spending more than it receives in taxation, will have to borrow money from investors either in this country or abroad. The amount of this borrowing is known as the Public Sector Borrowing Requirement. The more the government has to borrow the greater the inflationary pressure.

If the government is receiving more in taxation than it is paying, then it is in a position to pay back some of the national debt. This repayment is known as the Public Sector Debt Repayment.

Money supply

The government has used a number of different indicators to show or describe money supply. Over the years the number of indicators has been reduced to three, M0, M2 and M4.

M0 or M nought indicates the notes and coins in circulation outside the Bank of England and the balance the commercial banks keep with the Bank of England. By controlling the amount of money available to lend, the government can control the banks' ability to lend, which in turn can be used to control inflation.

M2 measures the money available to be spent immediately. This includes bank and building society accounts with less than one month to maturity.

M4 shows the total amount of private sector holdings of money in notes and coins, bank and building societies deposits and any other interest bearing accounts.

REVISION QUESTIONS – CHAPTER 14

1 Technical analysis is a study of supply and demand.   T F

2 A bar chart uses only the underlying security's closing   T F
price.

3 A support level is formed when supply outweighs   T F
demand.

4 A head and shoulders pattern can form at the bottom of   T F
a trend.

5 Moving averages should not be used as stop loss levels.   T F

6 Fundamental analysis uses management accounts to   T F
produce ratios and percentages.

7 The earning per share ratio can show the loss each share has made.   T F

8 The price/earnings ratio will show the number of years at the present earnings needed to cover the current market price.   T F

9 Dividends can not be paid out of reserves.   T F

10 Technical analysis and fundamental analysis can not be used together.   T F

Part Three

ADDITIONAL INFORMATION

15

OTHER DERIVATIVE INSTRUMENTS

While this book has concentrated on UK equity traded options for private investors, there are a number of other derivative instruments available to private investors and professionals, both in this country and abroad.

FUTURES

A futures contract is an agreement to buy or sell an asset on a fixed date in the future at a price agreed today.

Unlike traded options both parties to a futures contract are obligated to buy or sell the asset on the expiry date unless the position is closed out. There is no facility to abandon a contract if the market moves against the investor, the exchange will automatically exercise the futures contract into the underlying asset which the investor is obligated to buy or sell.

The potential loss of an investor who buys a futures contract is not limited to the initial amount paid as in traded options (Fig. 15.1). The buyer of a future pays a deposit (known as *initial margin*), which is only a fraction of the value of the contract, against his liabilities. As the market moves, the value of the day's gains or losses is added to or subtracted from the margin account. If the margin account has been added to, the money is paid out to the investor; if money has been subtracted from the account (to pay the counter party to the futures trade) the account must be 'topped up' on a daily basis. This system is known as *variation margin* with the futures contract being *marked to market*. The actual payment for the underlying asset does not take place until the futures contract is exercised.

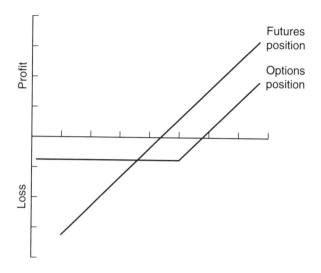

Figure 15.1   Long futures position v. long call position

An investor who has purchased a futures contract is obliged to buy the underlying asset and is known as being long of the future. An investor who has sold a futures contract is obliged to sell the underlying asset in the future and is known as being short of the future.

Delivery dates

Most futures have the same expiry cycle, known as delivery dates. It is during the delivery months that the underlying asset of the futures contract may by bought or sold. Although there is only one expiry cycle to cover all financial futures each contract will expire on a different day within each cycle. The cycle is:

March   June   Sept   Dec

Deliver dates may extend out to two or more years giving eight or more delivery dates.

Futures are available on a number of underlying assets ranging from crude oil, gold and financial instruments. We will just look at the use of stock index futures.

Hedging

Financial futures can be used in much the same way as traded options to speculate or to hedge. A hedge is a position in a derivative product (futures) whose rise in value will offset any loss in the underlying asset and can be used to reduce the risk of an adverse price movement in interest rates, exchange rates or market prices.

Example

On 10 January a fund manager is concerned about a possible rise in the equity market before 1 March when he will receive £5m to purchase a portfolio of equities.

To protect his purchasing powers the fund manager plans to buy the FT–SE 100 futures contract to cover any possible rise. The FT–SE 100 futures contract is priced in line with the FT–SE 100 index. Each index point represents £25, with a minimum price movement of 0.5 which is valued at £12.50. The minimum price movement is known as a 'tick'. With the March FT–SE 100 futures contract priced 3100 the fund manager needs 65 contracts to hedge his position.

Value of funds/((index level/tick size) × tick value)
5,000,000/((3100/0.5) × £12.50) = 64.5

On 1 March the FT–SE 100 share index has risen to 3317. The value of the planned portfolio has now risen to £5.35m; however the value of the futures contract has risen to £5.35m covering the increase of the stock market.

Stock market	**Trading**
	Futures market
10 Jan	Buy 65 FT–SE 100 futures
Value of planned portfolio	contracts at 3100 (value £5m)
£5m	

1 March	Sell 65 FT–SE 100 fuutres
Value of planned portfolio	contracts at 3317 (value
£5.35m	£5.35m)
	Gain ((3317–3100)/0.5) x
Extra cost £0.35m	£12.50 × 65 = £0.35m

Futures can be used for trading or speculation purposes in much the same way as traded options. Instead of buying futures to act as a hedge and offset a fall in the underlying asset, an investor trading in futures will buy or sell futures contracts hoping to sell the contracts or buy them back at a profit at a later date.

The advantage of trading in futures is that the investor does not have to own the underlying asset, coupled with only having to supply initial margin helping cash flow. Financial futures are a very attractive form of investment, especially for banks and financial institutions who have large exposure to interest and exchange rates.

WARRANTS

Warrants are issued by a company giving the holder the right to subscribe for a given number of shares, in the issuing company, at a previously agreed price. They are securities in their own right and as such are traded on the London Stock Exchange in exactly the same way as any other security. The holder, however, is not entitled to any dividends and the warrant has no voting rights. Warrants are not considered to be part of the company's issued share capital, but they do threaten to dilute it if and when they are exercised.

The company benefits from the issue of warrants by being able to use the proceeds of the sale for whatever purpose it sees fit, with no interest or dividend payments. If the warrant is not exercised by its expiry date it ceases to exist and becomes worthless.

Paying no dividends or interest means that any gain with warrants is in the form of capital gain, and as such is of particular interest to high rate taxpayers. They also offer a highly geared opportunity to make the capital gains. When the underlying security price is at £1 a

TRADITIONAL OPTIONS

First Dealings	Nov. 22	Last Declarations	Feb. 24
Last Dealings	Dec. 3	For settlement	March 7

3-month call rate indications are shown in Saturday editions.

Calls: **Aminex, Amstrad, Electron Hse., Glenchewton, Hanson Wts., Kewill Systems, Latham (J.), Minmet, Molyneux, Navan Res., Selec TV, Signet, Tuskar Res.** Puts: **Glenchewton, Kewill Systems, Tiphook, Transfer Tech.** Puts & Calls: **Aminex, Amstrad, Avesco, Navan Res., Smithkline Beech. A.**

Figure 15.2   Traditional options information from the FT

warrant with a subscription price of 90p will be worth at least 10p. A 10 per cent or 10p rise in the underlying security will result in a 10p or 100 per cent increase in the value of the warrant.

Pricing of warrants

A warrant is the equivalent of a long date call option and as such is priced in very much the same way. The underlying security and the subscription price of the warrant will determine its intrinsic value. The amount over and above the warrant's intrinsic value is its time value. Time value on a warrant will normally be considerably more than on a traded option due to the warrant's longer life and is therefore much harder to calculate.

TRADITIONAL OPTIONS

Traditional options have been traded on the London Stock Exchange for some considerable time. A traditional option can be taken out on any share listed on the London Stock Exchange and simply allows the investor to buy or sell the underlying security some time in the future at today's price.

Unlike traded options, traditional options cannot be traded in any circumstances. The strike or exercise price is *cum all*, that is to say, when the option is exercised any dividends paid by the company during the life of the option belong to the holder of the option (who is

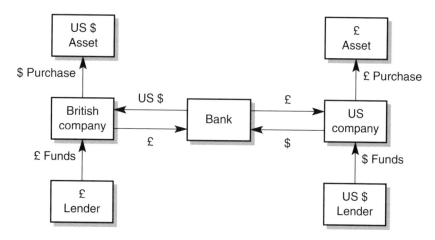

Figure 15.3 SWAPS

also known as the giver). The strike price is fixed at the time the option is taken out and is always the current underlying security price at the time of the agreement. Other differences between traded and traditional options are in the time of payment, the life of the option and declaration or exercise of the option.

Payment for traditional options is made on the Stock Exchange account day for the account that exercise or abandonment takes place in. The maximum life of a traditional option is seven account days which is equivalent to 14 weeks. Declaration day is when traditional options can be exercised and is the last but one dealing day in any account period during the life of the option. The declaration (exercise) must be made by 14.45 (Fig. 15.2).

Traditional options are available, providing an investor can find a counter party, on all securities traded on the London Stock Exchange except Gilts.

The disadvantage of traditional options is their inflexibility. Their life is restricted to seven account days, the strike or exercise price is limited to the price of the underlying security at the time of the agreement, and possibly the most restricting feature is not being able to trade out of the position.

OVER THE COUNTER OPTIONS (OTC)

In addition to exchange traded derivative products there is a large and fast growing market of over the counter options. These products are traded directly between investment firms, banks and their clients.

Whereas exchange traded products are standardised as to quantity, quality and life span to aid trading and settlement, OTC products are tailor made to suit each investor. This means they can be for odd numbers, an unusual or obscure security and for a life exceeding the normal nine months for an equity traded option. While this may sound like the perfect answer to every investor's dreams, unfortunately there are drawbacks to OTC options.

The liquidity and the ability to close out an option, or to give it its technical term, its *fungibility*, is a major disadvantage of OTC products. The only party an investor may close out an OTC option with is the original counter party. This may present problems if they do not wish to do so. The other alternative is to enter into a second option agreement, with a third party, which gives the investor an opposite position on the original terms.

The OTC market is not as rigorously supervised or regulated as exchange traded products.

SWAPS

SWAPS are an exchange of debt commitments between two parties and may be:

- Interest rates
- Currency exchange
- Index performance.

An example is of two companies, one British and one American. The British company has easy access to funds in sterling but has a commitment in US dollars. The American company on the other hand has easy access to funds in US dollars but has a commitment in pounds sterling.

The British company raises funds in sterling which it then SWAPS for the funds raised by the US company in US dollars (Fig. 15.3).

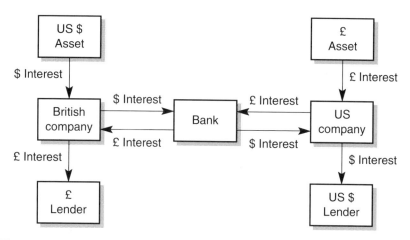

Figure 15.4 Interest payments

The British company now has a liability in sterling (to pay the interest on the funds it has raised) but an asset in US dollars, whereas the US company has a liability in US dollars and an asset in pounds sterling (Fig. 15.3). The two companies now have an exposure to movements in the exchange rate. An increase in the strength of the pound against the dollar will hurt the British company, whereas a rise in the dollar against the pound will hurt the US company. The British company pays the interest from its US dollar asset to the American company to pay its interest payment liability and the American company pays the interest from its sterling asset to the British company to pay its sterling interest payment liability (Fig. 15.4).

In between the two companies, arranging the SWAP and interest payments would usually be a bank or financial institution who will charge for their services.

LONDON DERIVATIVE EXCHANGES

UK equity options are traded on LIFFE which also trades financial futures and options, making it the largest derivatives exchange in Europe. However, there are a number of other derivative exchanges in London which deserve a mention.

The International Petroleum Exchange (IPE)

The IPE was established in 1981 to manage the risks associated with energy products. Its first contract was a futures contract on gas oil. Since then futures contracts on Brent crude oil and unleaded gasoline, along with traded options on the different futures, have become well established.

As with most exchanges IPE is a non-profit making exchange owned and run by its members. Each member must own or lease a 'seat' or share. Each seat entitles the owner to up to four traders on the market floor. The membership structure of the exchange consists of three main groups:

- Floor members can trade for their own account and on behalf of other IPE members and private clients
- Local members are entitled to trade on their own behalf or on behalf of other IPE members but not for private clients
- Trade associate members of the exchange are not allowed to trade on the market floor but have a representation on the IPE Board of Directors due to their interests in production, manufacture or distribution of oil and its by-products.

The IPE is a Recognised Investment Exchange (RIE) under the Financial Services Act 1986. As such it is regulated by the Securities and Investment Board with its members regulated by the Securities and Futures Authority.

Products
Futures
Gas oil
Brent crude oil
Options
Gas oil (Futures contract)
Brent crude (Futures contract)
Dubai crude oil.

London Commodity Exchange (formerly London Fox)

The product range of LCE falls into two groups; soft commodities and agricultural products with the one exception of the Baltic International Freight Futures Index. Following a restructure of the exchange there are four categories of exchange membership:

- Authorised Floor Members(clearing and non-clearing)
- Exchange Trade (cocoa) Membership
- Exchange Associate Membership
- Local Floor Membership.

LCE trade futures and options on all of the following except lamb which has just a futures contract.

Products
Cocoa
Robusta coffee
Raw sugar
White sugar
High protein soya bean meal
Grain
Pig
Potato
Freight (BIFFEX)
Lamb

London Metal Exchange (LME)

The LME is unusual in that there is no continuous trading throughout the day. Trading on the trading floor (ring) begins at 11.50a.m. when each metal trades in turn for five minutes. This continues until each metal has traded once. There is then a ten-minute break before each metal trades for a second time. At the end of the second trading session the settlement and official price for the day is established.

At the end of the morning session trading takes place in all six metals simultaneously outside of the ring. This is known as kerb trading.

One afternoon trading session, in the same format as the morning sessions, takes place, but without the establishment of a settlement or official price.

Products
Copper
Aluminium
Zinc
Tin
Lead
Nickel

OMLX The London Securities and Derivatives Exchange

While OMLX is a Recognised Investment Exchange with offices in London, it was originally established to trade futures and options on Swedish stocks to escape Swedish tax laws. It now intends to list and trade futures and options on UK stocks.

Trading is by means of a real time electronic dealing system between London and Stockholm. Prices are entered into the system from both locations with the best prices being calculated and distributed to all traders with a terminal. There are two categories of membership:

- Brokers, who trade on behalf of their clients, must be members of OMLX and the SFA
- Market makers, who are members of both OMLX and SFA, must quote continuous two-way prices for at least ten contracts, the series they are responsible for.

16

THE LONDON CLEARING
HOUSE AND MARGIN

All trades conducted on LIFFE, once checked and matched, need to be registered with a clearing house. It is the clearing house's responsibility to hold a register of all trades until the position is either closed or abandoned at expiry. Once registration has taken place the original counter party agreement is broken and replaced with an agreement between the counter parties and the clearing house. This process, known as novation, has two important consequences. First, any counter party credit risk is with the clearing house not an individual or a firm who may not be considered a good risk. Second, with the clearing house being at the centre of all trades, it allows a secondary market to be established allowing options to be traded freely and openly.

The clearing house for all trades on LIFFE is the London Clearing House (LCH) which, as part of the International Commodities Clearing House (ICCH), is a Recognised Clearing House under the FSA 1986. Under the FSA a clearing house must have:

1 Adequate financial resources.
2 Monitoring and compliance procedures.
3 High standards of integrity and fair dealing.
4 Co-operate with the Treasury and other regulators.

Membership of LCH (Fig. 16.1) is restricted to clearing members. These are firms who settle their own options business as well as being able to clear option business on behalf of other firms who are not members of LCH. Non- clearing members, usually small firms who do not transact sufficient business to justify the capital requirements of full membership of LCH, have an arrangement with clearing members for the clearing and settlement of their options business.

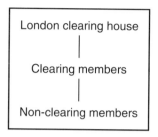

Figure 16.1 LCH membership

In addition to acting as the registrar and counter party to all trades, LCH calculates and holds margin. Margin, in the form of securities or cash, ensures that a writer of options can, if exercised against, take delivery of, or deliver the underlying security. LCH use a system called London SPAN to calculate margin requirements. SPAN (Standard Portfolio Analysis of Risk) was developed by the Chicago Mercantile Exchange (CME) and adapted by LCH to meet LIFFE's requirements. The result is London SPAN.

London SPAN constructs a risk array of sixteen different scenarios for changes in the price of the underlying security and in volatility (Table 16.1).

The range is the largest move in the price of the underlying security that the clearing house has identified as being likely in one day. For example the scanning range set for ABC Ltd might be 45 points. Therefore if ABC Ltd is trading at 330 the 3/3 up range would go up to 375.

The volatility range is set to cover any change that might be expected in one day. If ABC Ltd has a volatility of 15 per cent the 'volatility up' scenario might value the option at 16 per cent volatility.

The extreme move, up and down, is twice the normal scanning range.

LCH, after consultation with LIFFE, set all the parameters, such as scanning range, volatility and extreme moves. The parameters may be changed at any time to take account of changing market conditions.

Margin for short option positions consists of initial margin (calculated by London SPAN) and Net Liquidation Value (NLV).

$$\text{Margin} = \text{Initial margin} + \text{NLV}$$

1	underlying security unchanged	volatility up
2	underlying security unchanged	volatility down
3	underlying security up 1/3 range	volatility up
4	underlying security up 1/3 range	volatility down
5	underlying security down 1/3 range	volatility up
6	underlying security down 1/3 range	volatility down
7	underlying security up 2/3 range	volatility up
8	underlying security up 2/3 range	volatility down
9	underlying security down 2/3 range	volatility up
10	underlying security down 2/3 range	volatility down
11	underlying security up 3/3 range	volatility up
12	underlying security up 3/3 range	volatility down
13	underlying security down 3/3 range	volatility up
14	underlying security down 3/3 range	volatility down
15	underlying security up extreme move (cover 35% of loss)	
16	underlying security down extreme move (cover 35% of loss)	

Table 16.1 SPAN margining scenarios

NLV is calculated using the closing premium price of the series and is a negative figure for short position and a positive figure for long positions. If the closing premium for a short options position is 33p the NLV will be £330 (premium × contract size).

Example

An investor is short 1 ABC Mar 360 call. The initial margin is calculated at –£97. The closing premium is 54p giving an NLV of –£540.

Total margin = Initial margin + NLV
      = £97 + £540
      = £637 debit

Margin is also calculated on long option positions. However, the maximum loss a holder of an option can sustain is the premium paid for the option. Margin on a long position is a positive figure; it is not paid to the holder but may be used to offset margin requirement on short position in an option portfolio.

Positions continue to be margined after the option has been exercised but before delivery takes place. This takes into account any price movement in the underlying security between exercise and payment for the stock. Delivery margin consists of contingent margin and initial margin. Contingent margin is calculated as the difference between the exercise price and the underlying security's closing price.

While LCH sets the minimum margin requirements, brokers often require additional cover from their clients. This additional cover reflects the client's credit risk and, since margin requirements can change daily, means the broker does not have to be continually approaching the client for additional cover. The broker can increase margin calls at any time, but may not reduce the client's margin requirement below that calculated by LCH. LCH accepts a number of forms of collateral for margin. These include:

1 Cash.
2 Certain UK shares.
3 UK Bank guarantees.
4 UK Treasury Bills.
5 UK Gilts.
6 £ Certificates of deposit.
7 US Treasury Bonds.
8 US Treasury Bills and Notes.
9 $ Certificates of Deposit.
10 German Government Bonds.
11 Italian Government Bonds.
12 Italian Treasury Bills.
13 Spanish Government Bonds.
14 Spanish Treasury Bills.

Any securities put up as collateral must be registered into a nominee company controlled by LCH. This gives LCH legal rights over the securities should any default happen. All types of securities put up as collateral are liable to discounting by LCH to ensure their true market and saleable value is used when calculating margin.

REVISION QUESTIONS – CHAPTER 16

1 Initial margin is calculated using London SPAN.   T F

2 Net Liquidation Value is calculated using the opening   T F
premium price of the series written.

3 Cash can be put up as collateral.   T F

4 Securities put up as collateral are discounted by LCH.   T F

5 Not all members of LIFFE have to be members of LCH.   T F

17

CORPORATE EVENTS

During the life of an option any corporate event on the underlying security will result in an alteration to the contract specification of the option. The most common corporate events which will be covered here are a capitalisation issue, a rights issue, a takeover and a stock suspension.

CAPITALISATION ISSUE (BONUS OR SCRIP ISSUE)

A capitalisation issue, also known as a bonus or scrip issue, is an issue of shares, to existing share holders, fully paid for out of company cash reserves. Historically, shares in British companies have been priced under £5, making them attractive to private investors. If a company's share price rises above £5 and the company has sufficient cash reserves, it may consider a capitalisation issue to help promote its shares to private investors. The issue is expressed as a ratio to the share holders' existing holding. The options contract specification will be adjusted on the issues ex-entitlement date. The adjustment is calculated as follows:

New contract size = old contract size X (1 +x/y)

New exercise price = old exercise price X 1/1+x/y

where x = bonus entitlement.
       y = proportion of existing holding.

Example 1

ABC Plc announces a one-for-four capitalisation issue. This means the company is issuing one new share for every four shares an investor holds. The new options contract size will be adjusted as follows:

$$1000 \times (1 + 1/4) = 1250$$

The option has exercise prices of 280, 300, 330, 360 these will be adjusted as follows:

$$280 \times 1/1+1/4 = 224$$

$$300 \times 1/1+1/4 = 240$$

$$330 \times 1/1+1/4 = 264$$

$$360 \times 1/1+1/4 = 288$$

Any new series introduced after the ex-entitlement date will represent an option on 1000 shares as per normal contract specifications. If, during the calculations, the result is a fraction of a share the fraction is rounded to a whole number.

MARGIN

The value of shares pledged as margin will be adjusted proportionately on the ex-entitlement date.

For example, if the issue was a one-for-one by ABC Plc then writers of traded option contracts with ABC Plc shares pledged as collateral would find the value of their shares halved and would be required to put up further margin to cover the deficiency. This could be done by pledging further shares in ABC Plc in respect of their new entitlement or by providing another form of collateral.

RIGHTS ISSUE

A rights issue is a method of a company raising capital, by offering its existing share holders the right to subscribe to a new issue of shares, in proportion to their existing share holding. The issue is described as a ratio to the investor's existing holding, e.g. 3 for 7. This gives the investor the right to purchase 3 new shares, at the subscription price, for every 7 he already holds. The subscription price is normally at a discount to the current market price of the underlying security. The first calculation to be made is for the theoretical ex-rights price. This is the price the underlying security should be trading at after the rights issue and is as follows:

$$\text{Theoretical ex-rights price} = \frac{m \times P(cum) + n \times PR}{n + m}$$

$$\text{New contract size} = 1000 \times \frac{P(cum)}{P(tex)}$$

$$\text{New exercise price} = \text{existing exercise price} \times \frac{P(tex)}{P(cum)}$$

Where

m = proportion of existing shares.

P(cum) = underlying security cum-rights price.

n = new shares to be subscribed for.

PR = rights price.

P(tex) = theoretical ex-rights price.

Example 2

XYZ Plc announces a 3 for 7 rights issue with a subscription price of 227. The day prior to the shares being declared ex-rights the cum rights price is 234.

The theoretical rights price is:

$$\frac{7 \times 234 + 3 \times 227}{7 + 3} = 232$$

The new contract size is:

$$1000 \times \frac{234}{232} = 1009$$

The new exercise prices are:

$$200 \times \frac{232}{234} = 198$$

$$220 = 218$$

$$240 = 238$$

$$260 = 258$$

The result is that the holder of an old 220 series call option will now be able to buy the underlying security at a price of 218 × contract size (£2199) virtually the same price as the original contract. The writer's position is that although he must now deliver more shares, they are at a lower price per share. If he is a share holder he will be able to participate in the rights issue, while if he is not a share holder in the underlying security he will be delivering the shares in the ex-rights form by purchasing them cheaply in the market.

The holder of a put option will now be able to sell 1009 shares at the reduced exercise price and the writer of a put option will be obliged to take delivery of 1009 shares at 218 instead of 1000 at 220.

TAKEOVERS

If a takeover is announced on a security, on which traded options are traded, and an option is exercised, the procedure will depend on whether the takeover offer has been declared 'wholly unconditional' or not. If the takeover offer is not wholly unconditional and an option is exercised, the underlying security is delivered in 'non-assented form'.

In the event of a takeover offer being declared wholly unconditional then the terms of delivery will be in accordance with a General Notice issued by the Exchange.

STOCK SUSPENSION

A stock suspension happens when the London Stock Exchange suspends the dealing and settlement of shares in a particular security. During a stock suspension a buyer may still submit an exercise notice, via his broker, to the London Clearing House (LCH). If it is possible to deliver the underlying security through the London Stock Exchange settlement system the settlement of the exercised option will take place on settlement day as usual. If it is not possible to deliver the underlying security through the London Stock Exchange's settlement system then settlement will take place as per instructions laid down by LCH. These terms and conditions will be issued by a General Notice by the Exchange (LIFFE).

In the event of any stock situation it is important that an investor knows what effect the event has or could have on his holding and the exercise procedures associated with it. If the investor is in any doubt as to his position or holding, his broker will be able to advise him as to the bearing of the event on his holding.

REVISION QUESTIONS – CHAPTER 17

1 A capitalisation issue is also known as a bonus issue.   T F

2 An investor has to pay for his entitlement during a   T F
scrip issue.

3 The subscription price of a rights issue is normally at a   T F
discount to the current share price.

4 If, during a takeover, with the offer declared 'wholly   T F
unconditional', an option is exercised, the underlying
security is in 'non-assented form'.

5 During a stock suspension an exercise notice may still   T F
be submitted.

18

OPTIONS IN PORTFOLIO MANAGEMENT

Having looked at the theory and practice of traded options we now need to look at their uses in an investor's portfolio. No two investment portfolios will be identical; personal and financial details differ from one person to another, therefore not all of the following will apply to every investor. Before we look at how to use options in a portfolio we need to review investment needs and portfolio planning.

When receiving either investment advice or assessing your own situation there are a number of areas to be considered. These include:

1 Personal details: age, family commitments, occupation, pension (state and private), aversion to risk.
2 Assets: house(s).
3 Income: salary and investment.
4 Liabilities: mortgage, bank loans, school fees.
5 Tax position: income and possible inheritance.
6 Investment objectives: if known.

Only once all of the above have been assessed can a complete investment objective be established and a portfolio constructed. An investor will benefit from having a record of the criteria and his investment objectives. As circumstances change, the validity of the objectives criteria should be checked and updated when necessary. A portfolio, once constructed, should be thought of as a living, breathing entity, something to be nurtured and cared for. After all, it is expected to take care of the investor later in life.

One major choice facing the investor is whether to go for capital growth, income or a mixture of the two (Fig. 18.1). A relatively young investor will look for capital growth. With a considerable time

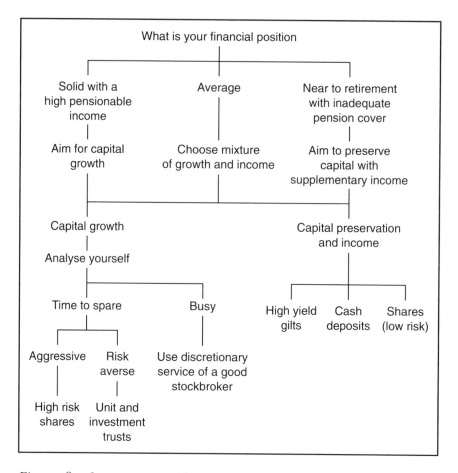

Figure 18.1 Investment considerations

before retirement he can afford to ride out any ups and downs in inflation and the equity market. His main consideration will be the amount of risk he is prepared to accept. On the other hand an investor approaching retirement will be concerned with capital preservation and generating income to supplement his pension.

INVESTMENTS AND RISK

As we have seen risk can be defined as either specific or non-specific in nature. Specific risk is associated with one particular company or share, whereas non-specific risk is connected with the economy and the equity market in general. Specific risk can be reduced to a minimum by holding a diversified portfolio of at least a dozen different shares from different market sectors. Non-specific risk on the other hand is far harder to counter.

Another way of looking at risk is to consider the likelihood of the value of the investment falling, or the risk of the issuer failing to honour its obligations.

No risk investments

Any investment issued by a reliable and respectable government. Gilts held to redemption.

Low risk

While there is no possibility of default, Gilts sold before redemption carry a risk of a fall in value.

Local authority stocks, deposits with high street banks and building societies, bonds issued by highly rated companies and life assurance policies all carry a low risk of default but a fall in value in real terms (after taking inflation into account) is a possibility.

Medium risk

Unit and investment trusts (collective investment schemes).

High risk

Equities and associated stock.
Warrants.

Very high risk

Futures.

Traded options have not been included in the list as the risk associated with them can be altered depending on how they are used and they can therefore fit into two or three of the categories. One thing that should be clear by now is the fact that traded options are only suitable for an investor with at least a holding in a collective investment scheme or an investor willing to accept a high degree of risk.

To illustrate the different ways options can be used as part of an overall investment objective we shall look at two different scenarios.

Investor 1

The first investor is a young single man with a secure, well-paid occupation offering health cover, pension (he also makes AVCs) and he owns his own home. While he has no equity portfolio at present he has spare cash and likes to take a risk. He now wishes to put a sum of money aside to invest in traded options.

His use of traded options should concentrate on their speculative or trading features, using the gearing effect to produce a high return. The profits gained from his use of options should be reinvested, not in the options market but elsewhere in a more secure investment vehicle such as a collective investment scheme (unit or investment trusts) or directly into equities.

Using options in this fashion the investor should be able to generate considerable returns without endangering more than the original amount set aside. This amount should be divided into units of a minimum of £500. When buying options no more than one unit should be used on one particular option. The golden rules for this investor must be to start off slowly after a period of ghost trading, not to commit too high a portion of the money set aside and always have a stop loss limit set.

Investor 2

The second investor is a mature and seasoned investor approaching retirement. He has paid off his mortgage, his family has grown up and left home and he has an equity portfolio.

His main objectives are to enhance the return from his portfolio while preserving the capital. These objectives, and the management of risk associated with his portfolio can be achieved with the use of traded options.

To enhance the returns from the portfolio the investor should consider writing covered call options on either individual stocks or on the FT–SE 100 index. The shares already owned can act as cover (margin) while the income received from the options premium will increase the overall portfolio return (Chapters 7 & 11).

To preserve the capital of the portfolio, buying puts on either individual stocks or the FT–SE 100 index should be considered. Buying puts will compensate for any fall in the value of the underlying securities and act as a hedge (Chapters 8 and 11).

INSTITUTIONAL USE

Institutions, such as pension funds and unit trusts, were initially slow to see the benefits of traded options. This was not helped by an unclear and ambiguous tax situation and a lack of experience in the use of traded options. In 1991 the Inland Revenue finally clarified the tax situation which opened up the options market to the large financial institutions. Now, virtually all large institutions use traded options in one way or another.

Using traded options gives institutions added flexibility, whether it is generating additional income or relocating assets at reduced transaction costs. One advantage an institution has over a private investor is the size and diversification of its portfolio which can be used as margin cover or to write options against. However, most are required to hold sufficient cash to cover all option positions by their trustees.

Institutions' main use of options is in efficient portfolio management; that is hedging and performance enhancement through writing options, rather than a speculative approach using the gearing effect.

Legislation in July 1991 allowed financial institutions to set up, run and market futures and options unit trusts in the UK. These funds fall into two categories; Futures and Options Funds (FOFs) or Geared Futures and Options Funds (GFOFs).

Futures and Options Funds are not permitted to undertake any trades that could result in profits from a geared position. These funds are unlikely to produce large profits for any investors. FOFs tend to be 'tracker' funds, that is they aim to produce the same returns as a particular index such as the FT–SE 100. In practice any fund manager who consistently tracks an index will outperform the competition.

Geared Futures and Options Funds are, as their names suggest, allowed to take geared positions in futures and options in order to produce large profits. Although geared positions are allowed, only 20 per cent of the funds' money is allowed to be invested in the futures and options market, with the remainder being invested in more secure investments, i.e. Gilts and on deposit. Although large profits are possible with GFOFs it is also possible, as with all unit trusts, to lose all the money invested.

FOFs and GFOFs are available to private investors, but the number of companies offering such funds is quite small to date. This is expected to change as the funds become accepted by private investors and regulators and fund managers gain experience of this type of fund.

19

REGULATION

All forms of investment within the UK are regulated under the Financial Services Act (FSA) 1986. The introduction of the FSA was instigated in 1982 by the Gower report on investor protection. The act defines investment as any right, asset or interest within the following groups:

1 Stocks and shares in the share capital of a company, excluding building societies.
2 Debentures and loan stock.
3 Government, local authority or public authority securities including foreign countries and organisations.
4 Warrants.
5 Certificate conferring the right to convert, acquire or dispose of a security.
6 Units in a collective investment scheme (unit and investment trusts).
7 Options to acquire or dispose of investments.
8 Futures on anything for investment purposes.
9 Contracts for difference (FT–SE 100 index futures and options).
10 Long-term insurance contracts.

Under the FSA anyone conducting investment business must be authorised. Investment business is defined as:

- Dealing in investments on behalf of others
- Arranging deals in investments on behalf of others
- Managing investments such as pension funds and discretionary accounts
- Giving advice on investments
- Setting up and running collective investment plans.

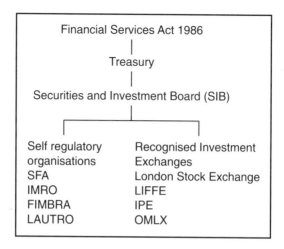

Figure 19.1 FSA power delegation

The act works by requiring any firm or person conducting investment business to be authorised by the appropriate body. Authorisation is dependent on two main conditions:

- The person must be *fit and proper*. The act does not define fit and proper but it is generally taken to mean the person must be solvent and with no criminal record.
- The company must have *capital adequacy*. This is designed to prevent a company with inadequate capital backing from using money belonging to clients to support the company.

The act also lays down *conduct of business rules* on the company's relationship with its clients whose interests should be put before those of the company.

The powers of the FSA have been delegated by the government to the **Securities and Investment Board (SIB)**. The SIB in turn has delegated some power to four **Self-Regulatory Organisations** and **Recognised Investment Exchanges (RIE)** (Fig. 19.1).

The four SROs which cover all aspects of investment within the UK are:

1 The Securities and Futures Authority (SFA). Firms involved in the securities industry, futures and options.

2 The Investment Management Regulatory Organisation (IMRO). Firms whose main business is fund management, i.e. pension funds, investment and unit trusts.

3 The Financial Intermediaries, Managers and Brokers Regulatory Association (FIMBRA). Independent intermediaries giving advice on and arranging deals in unit trusts and life assurance.

4 The Life Assurance and Unit Trust Regulatory Organisation (LAUTRO). Firms marketing life assurance and unit trusts.

The system works on a three-tier principle:

- 10 general principles, written by the SIB but applicable to all SROs
- Approximately 40 core rules, written by the SIB in consultation with the SROs. They are also applicable to all SROs
- Detailed rules and codes of practice written by and for each individual SRO.

All SROs are required to have in place rules and procedures regarding the following:

- Members to be fit and proper
- Admission, expulsion and discipline
- Safeguards for investors
- Monitoring and enforcement of rules
- Investigating complaints
- Promotion and maintenance of standards.

Certain individuals, while allowed to conduct investment business, are not regulated by any of the four self-regulatory bodies. This group of people belong to **Recognised Professional Bodies (RPB)**. This allows professional people such as accountants and solicitors to give investment advice to their clients. Under the FSA each RPB must limit the amount of investment business their members undertake. Other exemptions to being a member of an SRO include:

- The Bank of England
- Lloyd's of London Insurance market and its agents
- Representatives of one company (life insurance and unit trust companies)

- Some listed money market institutions which are regulated by the Bank of England
- Recognised Investment Exchanges.

SECURITIES AND FUTURES AUTHORITY (SFA)

Under the SFA's conduct of business rule all SFA registered firms must deal with clients' orders as soon as reasonably practical and may not delay the execution of the order, unless they believe the delay is in the best interest of the client.

When dealing, the firm must ensure that it transacts all client business at the best price available in the market. This requirement is also covered by the London Stock Exchange rules on 'best execution'.

Where an investor relies on the firm to give investment advice (advisory service), or deal on behalf of an investor (discretionary service), a firm may not recommend or deal for an investor if the deal could be regarded as too frequent. This is to stop the firm dealing just to earn commission for itself. This type of dealing is known as 'churning'.

Each firm must have adequate internal procedures to ensure members of staff do not breach any SIB, SFA or FSA rules and regulations. To oversee this requirement each firm has a compliance officer. It is their responsibility to inspect company and client records for irregularities.

RECOGNISED INVESTMENT EXCHANGES

All investment markets in the UK are authorised under the FSA as either Recognised Investment Exchanges (RIE), or alternatively, foreign or international exchanges can be recognised as a Designated Investment Exchange (DIE). An investment exchange is a company or organisation that provides a structured and co-ordinated market place where investment business is conducted. The exchange must ensure that there are adequate means for the establishment and dissemination of investment prices and for supervising market activities. They must also have provision for dealing with complaints and illegal market activities.

A DIE, while not under direct control of the SIB, is acknowledged as being regulated in an appropriate manner by its domestic regulator.

Membership of an investment exchange does not grant the right of an individual, or a firm, to conduct investment business; that right can only be granted by an SRO or the SIB. Membership of a RIE allows the individual or firm to conduct investment business on that exchange once authorised by an SRO or the SIB.

Risk warning

A requirement of the SFA in its regulation of the futures and options markets is its risk warning letter. The letter sets out the risk associated with different aspects of options trading and must be read, signed and returned to a broker before he can:

- Recommend a trade
- Arrange or execute a trade whether it was his recommendation or not
- Act as discretionary manager.

REVISION QUESTIONS – CHAPTER 19

1 All forms of investment in the UK are regulated by the Financial Services Act 1986.   T F

2 Giving financial advice is not covered by the FSA.   T F

3 A person may be authorised to conduct investment business if he is bankrupt.   T F

4 A broking firm operating a discretionary service for a client may deal on his behalf to generate extra commission for themselves.   T F

5 A risk warning letter must be signed and returned to a broker before dealing can commence.   T F

20

ADVANCED OPTIONS PRICING THEORIES

In Chapter 5 we looked at the variables that are used in a pricing model to calculate the fair value of an option. In this chapter we look at some of the reasons for the outcome and at options sensitivities.

EXPECTED RETURNS, THEORETICAL VALUE AND VOLATILITY

The possibility of any outcome for a share price during the life of an option can be shown by a normal distribution curve (Fig. 20.1). The curve is peaked in the centre (highest return possibility) with flared tails (the right- hand tail shows the possibility of a maximum return while the left-hand tail shows the possibility of a minimum return).

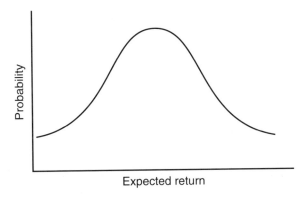

Figure 20.1 Normal distribution curve

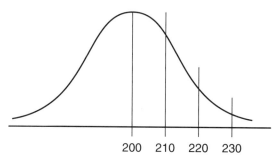

Figure 20.2 Normal distribution curve price areas

If the normal distribution curve is divided into price ranges (Fig. 20.2) the proportion of an area (200–210) to the total area (160–240) will represent the probability that the underlying security will fall between the prices (200–210) at the expiry of the option.

The area 200–210 represents 20 per cent of the total area of 140–240. Therefore there is a 20 per cent chance of the underlying security being between 200–210 when the option expires. This probability can be used when calculating the expected return of an option (Table 20.1 and Fig. 20.3). If an investor has purchased a 200 call option his expected return can be calculated as follows:

Price range	Mid price	Probability	Expected profit
200–210	5	20%	1
210–220	15	15%	2.25
220–230	25	10%	2.5
230–240	35	5%	1.7

		Expected profit	7.5

Table 20.1 Expected profit

This information can also be shown in a linear form (Fig. 20.3). (With a call option giving the right to buy the underlying security, the only downside risk is the premium paid for the option.) With the 200

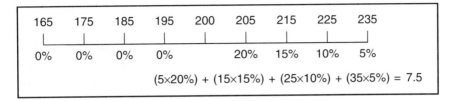

165	175	185	195	200	205	215	225	235
0%	0%	0%	0%		20%	15%	10%	5%

(5×20%) + (15×15%) + (25×10%) + (35×5%) = 7.5

Figure 20.3 Expected return

call option having an expected profit of 7.5 an investor would expect to make a profit if he can purchase the option for less than 7.5p. This expected profit is better known as the theoretical value of an option.

Most pricing models assume that the possible prices of an option are distributed along a normal distribution curve. The normal distribution curve and the price areas in Fig. 20.2 are a very simplified example. In a pricing model the formula would calculate the expected returns for each price point 200, 201, 202, etc.

The rate at which a normal distribution curve spreads out is associated with the volatility of the underlying security (Fig. 20.4). A security with a low volatility will have a normal distribution curve that is very tall with short tails. Medium volatility will show a normal distribution curve still peaked in the centre, but not to the same extent as the low volatility, with longer tails than the low volatility curve. A security with high volatility will have a flat normal distribution curve with long tails spreading out over a greater price range.

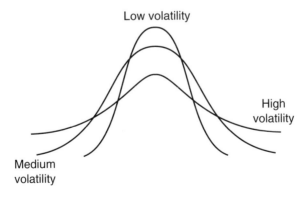

Figure 20.4 High, low and medium volatility and normal distribution curves

These normal distribution curves show that a low volatility stock has the greater probability of attaining its expected return with only small chances of either high or low returns. A stock with medium volatility has a high probability of attaining its expected returns, but the opportunity for higher or lower returns has increased. A security with high volatility has a decreased chance, when compared with either the low or medium volatility stocks, of attaining its expected return but the opportunity for very high or very low returns has increased.

The rate at which a normal distribution curve spreads out from the centre or mean is known as its standard deviation. The exact standard deviation figures are found in mathematical tables, but as a rough guide:

+/– one standard deviation will take in 68% of all outcomes.

+/– two standard deviation will take in 95% of all outcomes.

+/– three standard deviation will take in 99% of all outcomes.

Once an investor knows and understands the theory of standard deviations it can be used in conjunction with the volatility of the underlying security to calculate the standard deviation for one week or one day. Volatility is usually expressed as a percentage over a year. With UK equity options having a maximum life of nine months it is more practical to express volatility and standard deviation in weekly and daily terms.

To calculate a weekly standard deviation the square root of the number of trading weeks in a year is required.

$$\sqrt{52} = 7.2$$

To calculate a daily standard deviation the square root of the number of trading days in a year is required.

$$\sqrt{256} = 16$$

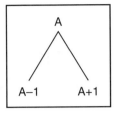

Figure 20.5 Binomial pricing

If a stock with traded options based on it is trading at 200 with a volatility of 15 per cent in one day's time an investor can expect it to be trading in a range of 198–202:

$$0.15/16 \times 200 = 2$$

and in one week's time he can expect it to be trading in a range of 196–204:

$$0.15/7.2 \times 200 = 4$$

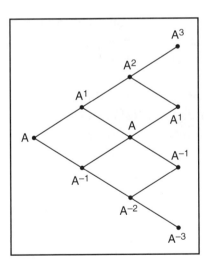

Figure 20.6 Binomial pricing tree

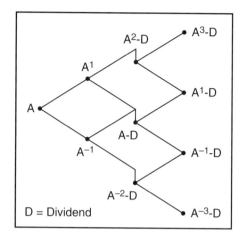

Figure 20.7 Pricing tree with dividend

Pricing models

The two main pricing models available are the Black and Scholes analogous model and the Cox, Ross and Rubenstein binomial model.

The Black and Scholes model was the first pricing model to be produced and allowed the options markets to be properly priced for the first time. The model is based on a non-dividend paying European option. It also assumes there are only two possible stock prices at the expiry of the option. This is obviously a very inaccurate picture of what does happen in reality.

A more realistic pricing model is the binomial pricing model first designed by Cox, Ross and Rubenstein. The binomial model is, in very simple terms, a model that consists of two options or choices at the end of each stage or time period, and can be drawn as a pricing tree. The life of the option is divided into a large number of small time periods. It is then assumed that the price of the underlying security can move up or down during the time period. In Fig. 20.5 the underlying security price starts from point A, from there it can go up or down in the given time.

From each of these outcomes, or price points, the prices can again rise or fall producing a further three price points. So the process continues over the life of the option (Fig. 20.6) until a pricing tree is produced.

Underlying security	Premium	Delta	New premium
345	25	.25	25.0
345	25	.5	25.5
345	25	1.0	26.0

Table 20.2 The effect of an options Delta

The time between each price point and the amount of price movement will determine if the stock has high, low or medium volatility. The prices of a stock with high volatility will move up or down much further in the same time scale as a stock with medium volatility. A stock with low volatility will move up or down much slower over a longer time scale.

When a dividend is paid on the underlying security the stock price will be reduced by the amount of the dividend. This can be shown in the pricing tree by a drop in all of the lines connecting the price points (Fig. 20.7).

Using a binomial pricing tree, option prices are calculated by starting at the end of the tree and working backwards. At the end of the tree the option is valued at its intrinsic value only. At any earlier price points the value of an option is the greater of:

1 The option's intrinsic value.

or

2 The value if held for a further period of time.

The option's intrinsic value is the amount the option is in-the-money. If the option is held for a further period of time its value is its expected value at the end of that period.

OPTIONS SENSITIVITY

Option prices, as we have discussed, are derived by a pricing formula and six variables. Not only will pricing formulas give the price of an option for any given combination of variables, they will also show how the price generated will change for a particular change in one of the variables. These changes are known by Greek letters and are referred to as options sensitivities.

Delta

The first and the most common of the options sensitivities is Delta. Call options have a positive Delta between 0 and 1, with 0 for deep out-of-the-money series and 1 for deep in-the-money series. Put options have negative Deltas and are between −1 and 0. Deltas can be explained in four ways.

1 The rate of change in an option's theoretical fair value for a one penny change in the underlying security's price. Table 20.2 shows how a call option premium changes for a 1p rise in the underlying security. Put premiums, with their Delta being negative, would go down for a rise in the underlying security.

The first series with a Delta of 0.25 is a deep out-of-the-money series. A 1p change in the underlying security will not affect the premium. The second series is at-the-money and has a Delta of 0.5. For every 1p change in the underlying security the premium of an at-the-money option will change at half the rate, i.e. 0.5. The last series with a Delta of 1 is a deep in-the-money option and for every 1p change in the underlying security there will be a 1p change in the premium.

2 The ratio of the underlying security to options contracts, required to establish a neutral hedge. Rather than buying stock 1–1 with option contracts as a hedge, for example, the seller of an option buys stock in the ratio indicated by the Delta value. If an investor sells 10 contracts with a Delta of 0.3, he would buy 3000 stock to hedge the position. If the investor purchased one call option with a Delta of 0.75 he would sell 750 shares in the underlying contract.

3 The theoretical share position for an options position. The holder of a call position is theoretically long of the underlying security, for a put position the holder is theoretically short. For example, if an investor buys a call option with a Delta of 0.25 he is theoretically

long 25 per cent of the underlying contract, 250 shares. This definition can also be referred to as the theoretical or equivalent share position.

4 Approximately the probability, given constant and stable volatility, that the option will expire in-the-money. An option with a Delta of 0.5 has a 50 per cent chance of expiring in-the-money. An option with a Delta of 0.9 has a 90 per cent chance.

An options Delta is not a constant figure but changes with every price movement of the underlying security. The amount by which it changes is known as the Gamma.

Gamma

The Gamma is the theoretical rate of change of an options Delta for a one penny change in the underlying security. For example if a call option has a Delta of 0.25 and a Gamma of 0.05 for a penny rise in the underlying security, the Delta will change to 0.30. For a one penny fall the Delta will be 0.20. The Gamma of an option is also known as its curvature.

The Delta of an option can be described as the speed with which an options premium moves, in respect to the changes in the underlying security price. The range of speed is from 0 per cent (for a deep out-of-the-money series) to 100 per cent (for a deep in-the-money series) or from 0–100 per cent for puts. Gamma can then be thought of as the rate of acceleration or deceleration of the Delta.

Theta

With options being a limited life security it is important to know how much theoretical value an option will lose for each day that passes with no movement in the underlying security. This theoretical loss in value for each day that passes is known as Theta. An option with a Theta of 0.005 will lose 0.005 in theoretical fair value for each day that passes with no movement in the underlying security. Theta is better known as time decay.

Vega

Volatility is a particularly important factor in the pricing of options. The sensitivity of an option's fair value to changes in its theoretical volatility is measured by its Vega. An option with a Vega of 0.75 would gain (lose) 0.75p for each percentage point increase (decrease) in volatility. Vega is also known as Kappa, Epsilon and Omega.

Rho

The sensitivity of an option's fair value to interest rate movements is measured by its Rho. An option with a Rho of 0.03 would gain (lose) 0.03p for each percentage point increase (decrease). Rho is the least important of all the option sensitivities.

APPENDICES

APPENDIX A

Answers

Chapter 2

1 *True.*
2 *False.* The holder of a call option has the right to purchase the underlying security at the exercise price. It is the holder of a put who has the right to sell.
3 *True.*
4 *True.*
5 *False.* The maximum life of an equity option is nine months.
6 *True.* The maximum loss a holder of an option can sustain is the premium paid for the option.
7 *False.* There are normally 1000 shares per contract.
8 *True.*
9 *False.* There are three expiry cycles:

1	Jan	Apr	Jul	Oct
2	Feb	May	Aug	Nov
3	Mar	Jun	Sep	Dec

10 *True.*

Chapter 3

1 *True.* The maximum loss, when purchasing an option, is the premium.
2 *False.* The break-even point is 192 (exercise price + premium).
3 *False.* The maximum profit when buying a call is unlimited. The maximum profit when selling a call is limited to the premium received.
4 *True.*
5 *False.* Put options give the holder the right to sell the underlying security. If the market is expected to rise the investor should buy call options allowing him to purchase stock below the current market value.
6 *False.* The maximum profit with a short call position is limited to the premium received.
7 *True.*
8 *False.* A put option gives the holder the right to sell the underlying security, therefore the seller of a put must take delivery of the underlying security if exercised against.

9 *True.* If the market is expected to rise the investor should buy call options allowing him to purchase stock below the current market value.
10 *True.*

Chapter 4

1 *False.* Index options are based on the FT–SE 100 share index.
2 *True.*
3 *True.* Index options are known as contracts for difference and are cash settled if exercised.
4 *False.* Each index point is worth £10.
5 *False.* European style options can only be exercised at expiry. American style options can be exercised any time during their life.

Chapter 5

1 *False.* There are six main variables:
 - Stock price
 - Exercise price
 - Time to expiry
 - Volatility
 - Interest rates
 - Dividends.
2 *True.*
3 *True.*
4 *False.* As an option nears expiry so its time value will decrease.
5 *True.*
6 *False.* Holders of options are not entitled to any dividend payments on the underlying security.
7 *False.* The price produced by a pricing model is the *fair price*. The market price is the fair price plus supply and demand and other factors.
8 *True.*
9 *False.* An increase in volatility will result in an increase in option premiums due to the increased movement in the underlying security.
10 *True.*
11 *True.*
12 *True.* An option with intrinsic value is known as in-the-money. An option with no intrinsic value is known as out-of-the-money. An option whose exercise price is equal to the u/s price is known as at-the-money.
13 *False.* With the underlying security price at 231 a 220 call option will have 11p intrinsic value.
14 *True.*
15 *True.* Time value represents the remaining life of the option and the possibility of price movements affecting the option's intrinsic value.

16

Share price 458

Exercise price	Call		Put	
	Intrinsic	*Time*	*Intrinsic*	*Time*
420	38	1	0	3
460	0	12	2	16
480	0	2	22	8

17 *True.*

18 *True.* With the rise in the underlying security being over a short period there will be no significant erosion of time value. Coupled with the increase in intrinsic value, or the potential for acquiring intrinsic value, will result in a large increase in premiums.

19 *True.*

20 *False.* Due to the gearing effect it is important to predict the extent and timing of any price movement.

Chapter 6

1 *True.*

2 *False.* When a rise in the underlying security is expected over a long period, in-the-money options should be purchased.

3 *False.* The investor should only use some of his profits in case the underlying security falls.

4 *False.* The maximum loss when purchasing calls is limited to the premium paid.

5 *True.* If there is time value attached to the option an investor should consider selling the option back into the market, realising both intrinsic and time value.

Chapter 7

1 *True.*

2 *False.* Uncovered or naked writing is the riskiest strategy available.

3 *True.*

4 *True.*

5 *True.*

6 *False.* Writing calls can be used to secure a selling price.

7 *True.*

8 *True.*

9 *False.* Check with your broker for a complete and up to-date list.

10 *False.* It is one of the riskiest strategies available.

Chapter 8

1 *False.* Puts should be purchased in the expectation of a fall in the underlying security.
2 *True.*
3 *True.*
4 *False.* Puts provide more downside protection than writing calls.
5 *False.* The investor will continue to participate in any rise in the underlying security, but at a slightly reduced rate due to the premium paid out for the position.

Chapter 9

1 *False.* A covered put writer holds cash in case of being exercised against.
2 *False.* All writers of options must submit margin.
3 *True.*
4 *True.*
5 *False.* A writer of put options is obliged to take delivery (buy) the underlying security.

Chapter 10

1 *True.*
2 *True.*
3 *True.*
4 *False.* A straddle involves the purchase of equal amounts of calls and puts.
5 *True.*
6 *True.*
7 *False.* A ratio call spread is constructed by purchasing one call at a low exercise price and selling two calls at a higher exercise price.
8 *True.*
9 *True.*
10 *True.*

Chapter 11

1 *True.*
2 *True.*
3 *False.* Call options will decrease in value as the underlying security price falls. To hedge a holding in the underlying security it is necessary to purchase put options.
4 *False.* The formula for constructing a simple hedge is:
Number of shares to be hedged/contract size.
5 *True.*

Chapter 12

1 *False.* The trading hours are 08.35–16.10.
2 *True.*
3 *True.*
4 *True.*
5 *False.* Payment must be to LCH by 10.00a.m. However, individual brokers will have their own timings.
6 *True.*
7 *False.* The selection procedure for selecting writers is by computerised random selection.
8 *True.*
9 *True.* But only on expiry days, otherwise it is 17.20.
10 *True.* But on expiry days this is extended to 18.00.
11 *True.*
12 *False.* A PLO is a firm dealing instruction and does not need to be confirmed before being dealt.
13 *False.* No conditions can be attached to a PLO.
14 *False.* PLOs can be withdrawn any time during trading hours. If they are dealt between the broker receiving instructions to cancel the PLO and withdrawing it from the market the deal will stand.
15 *False.* Less than 1 per cent of business on LIFFE is conducted through the PLOB.

Chapter 13

1 *False.* All brokers must be members of the Securities and Futures Authority.
2 *True.*
3 *True.*
4 *False.* A discretionary service is the most expensive. The cheapest service is an execution only service.
5 *False.* Brokers are not informed of any ghost trades conducted.

Chapter 14

1 *True.*
2 *False.* A bar chart is constructed using the high, low, close prices. A line chart will use just the closing price.
3 *False.* A support level is where demand outweighs supply forcing the price higher.
4 *True.*
5 *False.* Moving averages can be used as a stop level.
6 *True.*
7 *True.*
8 *True.*

9 *False.*

10 *False.* If an investor finds it helpful to combine technical and fundamental analyses in choosing stocks there is nothing wrong with it.

Chapter 16

1 *True.*

2 *False.* NLV is calculated using the closing premium price.

3 *True.*

4 *True.*

5 *True.*

Chapter 17

1 *True.*

2 *False.* A scrip issue is a full paid-up issue of new shares to existing share holders.

3 *True.*

4 *False.* If a takeover is declared 'wholly unconditional' and an option is exercised the underlying security will be delivered in accordance with a General Notice issued by the exchange.

5 *True.*

Chapter 19

1 *True.*

2 *False.* Giving investment advice is covered by the FSA.

3 *False.* All individuals conducting investment business must be solvent.

4 *False.*

5 *True.*

APPENDIX B

Contract specifications

All traded options contracts are standardised to allow easy trading on a market floor. This means there is no lengthy and time-consuming negotiation about what is being traded, the life of the option or its exercise price.

Type of Option	UK Equity Options	FT–SE 100 (American Exercise)	FT–SE 100 (European Exercise)
Based On	Ordinary shares of 73 Leading UK companies + 1 SA company	Financial Times – Stock Exchange 100 Index	Financial Times – Stock Exchange 100 Index
Normal Contract Size	1000 shares (Vaal Reefs = 100 shares)	Index Value × £10	Index Value × £10
Expiry Cycle	1 Jan, Apr, Jul, Oct. 2 Feb, May,Aug,Nov. 3 Mar, Jun, Sep, Dec.	Nearset four Months Plus June and Dec.	Mar, Jun, Sept, Dec Plus two additional Near Months.
Maximum Life	9 Months	12 Months	12 Months
Exercise Times	Until 17.20 on any Business Day. Extended to 18.00 on Any Last Trading Day.	16.31 on any Business Day. Extended to 18.00 on the Last Day of Trading.	18.00 only on Expiry Day.
Expiry Day & Time	16.10. Normally Two Days Before Last Day Of Dealing For Last Complete Stock Exchange Account Of Expiry Month.	10.30. Third Friday Of The Expiry Month.	10.30 Third Friday Of The Expiry Month.
Quotation	Pence Per Share	Index Points	Index Points
Trading Hours	08.35–16.10	08.35–16.10	08.35–16.10

APPENDIX C

Option stockbrokers for private investors

Company	Address/ Tel No	Minimum Account £	Commission & Charges	Services Offered
ALBERT E SHARP & CO	Edmund House, 12 Newhall Street, Birmingham B3 3ER 021 200 2244	None	Open £30 Close £10 £1.40/contract Scale – Opening: 4% first £1000 2% next 5000 1% on balance. Half above fees on closing	Discretionary, Advisory and Execution
ALLIED PROVINCIAL SECURITIES	St Catherine's House, Notte Street, Plymouth PL1 2TW 0752 220971	Adequate fund to cover purchases	£29.50 min. £2.50/contract Scale – 2.5% first £5000, 1% on remainder. £10 exercise /assignment	Discretionary, Advisory and Execution
ALLIED PROVINCIAL SECURITIES	City House, 206–208 Marton Rd, Middlesbro. TS4 2JE 0642 249211	Adequate fund to cover purchases	£29.50 min. £2.50/contract Scale – 2.5% first £5000, 1% on remainder. £10 exercise /assignment	Discretionary, Advisory and Execution
BELL LAWRIE WHITE & CO	7 Drumsheugh Gardens, Edinburgh EH3 7QH 031 225 2566	None	£30 min. £2/ contract Scale – 1.85% first £10,000 1% next £20,000 0.25% on remainder	Execution

Company	Address/ Tel No	Minimum Account £	Commission & Charges	Services Offered
BROWN SHIPLEY STOCK-BROKING	30–31 Friar Street, Reading RG1 1AH 0734 595511	None	£30 min. £2.50/ contract £5/ contract note Scale – 2.5% first £5000 1.5% next £5000 1% on remainder	Execution some Advisory
CAVE & SONS	PO Box 32, 9–11 Hazelwood Rd, Northampton NN1 1LQ 0604 21421	Sufficient funds to cover purchase	£25 min. £2/ contract Scale – 2% first £5000 1% on remainder	Execution
CAWOOD SMITHIE & CO	20 Strathview Park, Netherlee, Glasgow G44 3LA 041 637 0000	Sufficient funds to cover purchase	£20 min. £2.25/ contract Scale – 2.5% first £5000 1.5% on remainder	Execution
CAWOOD SMITHIE & CO	25 East Parade, Harrogate, Yorkshire HG1 5LT	Sufficient funds to cover purchase	£20 min. £2.25/ contract Scale – 2.5% first £5000 1.5% on remainder	Execution
CENTRAL STOCK-BROKING SERVICES LIMITED	86 King Street, Manchester M2 4WQ 061 832 2924	None	£40 min. £1.40/contract 0.05% clearing fee – Scale – 3.5% first £5000 2% next £5,000 1.25% on remainder	Discret-ionary, Advisory and Execution
CHARTER HOUSE TILNEY	The Royal Liver Building, Liverpool L3 1NY 051 236 6000	None	£34 min. £1.60/ contract Scale – 2.5% first £5000 1.5% next £5000 0.5% on remainder	Advisory and Execution

Company	Address/ Tel No	Minimum Account £	Commission & Charges	Services Offered
CHRISTOWS	The Lodge 10a Southernhay West Exeter EX1 1JG 0392 210510	None	£30 min. £2/ contract Scale – 2.5% first £5000 1.5% next £5000 1% on remainder	Advisory and Execution
DERIVATIVE SECURITIES	1 Briset Street London EC1M 5NR 071 253 5835	£2500	£37.50 min. £2/ contract Scale – 2% first £5000 1.5% next £5000 1% on remainder	Discret- ionary, Advisory and Execution
DURLACHER & CO	10 Throgmorton Avenue London EC2N 2DL 071 628 4306	£500	£25 min. £2/ contract £7 com- pliance charge per bargain Scale – 2% first £5000 1% remainder	Discret- ionary, Advisory and Execution
FAIRMONT STOCK- BROKERS	Huntingdon House Princess Street Bolton BL1 1EJ 0204 362233	£500	£30 min. £2.50/ contract Scale – 1.95%	Advisory and Execution
FLEMING PRIVATE ASSET MANAGE- MENT	31 Sun Street London EC2M 2QP 071 377 9242	None	£35 min. £1.5/ contract Scale – 2.5% first £5000 1.5% next £5000 1% on remainder Half commission on closing	Discret- ionary, Advisory and Execution
GNI	4th Floor Altrium Building Cannon Bridge 25 Downgate Hill London EC4R 2GN 071 337 3500	£10,000	£30 min. 60p/ contract Scale – 2.5%	Advisory and Execution

Company	Address/ Tel No	Minimum Account £	Commission & Charges	Services Offered
HARRIS ALLDAY LEA & BROOKS	33 Great Charles Street Birmingham B3 3JN 021 233 1222	£1000	£25 min. £2.50/ contract £5 admin fee Scale – 2.5% opening Half commission on closing	Advisory and Execution
HENRY COOKE LUMSDEN	1 King Street PO Box 369 Manchester M60 3AH 061 834 2332	None	£30 min. £2.00/ contract Scale – 2.5% first £5000 1.5% next £5000	Advisory and Execution
HILL OSBORNE & CO	Permanent House Horsefair St Leicester LE1 5BU 0533 629185	None	£30 min. £1.40/ contract Scale – 2.5% first £5000 1.5% remainder	Execution
JAMES BREARLY & SONS	56–60 Caunce Street Blackpool FY1 3DQ 0253 21474	None	£22 min. £2/ contract Scale – 2% first £5000 1% remainder	Discret-tionary, Advisory and Execution
KILLIK & CO	24–25 Manchester Sq. London W1M 5AP 071 224 2050	None	£30 min. £2.25/ contract Scale – 2% first £5000 1.5% next £5000 1% remainder	Discret-ionary, Advisory and Execution
NICHOLSON BARBER & CO	PO Box 132 New Oxford House, Barkers Pool, Sheffield S1 1LE 0742 755100	Sufficient funds to cover purchase	£17 min. £2/ contract Scale – 1.25% first £10,000 0.5% next £10,000	Advisory and Execution
NICHOLSON BARBER & CO	Cameron House 9 Thorne Rd Doncaster DN1 2HP 0302 320322	None	£17 min. £2/ contract Scale – 1.25% first £10,000 0.5% next £10,000	Advisory and Execution

Company	Address/ Tel No	Minimum Account £	Commission & Charges	Services Offered
QUILTER GOODISON COMPANY	Exchange House Primrose Street London EC2A 2NR 071 606 8022	Sufficient funds to cover purchase	£37 min. £1.50/ contract £3 per bargain Scale – 2.25% first £5000 1.5% next £5000 1% on remainder	Execution
RAPHEAL ZORN HEMSELY	10 Throgmorton Avenue London EC2N 2DP	£1000 buying £10,000 writing	£40 min. £1.70/ contract Scale – 2.25% first £10,000 1% on remainder	Discret- ionary, Advisory and Execution
REDMAYNE BENTLEY	Merton House 84 Albion Street Leeds LS1 6AG 0532 436941	£500	£17.50 min. £1.40/contract Scale – 2.5% first £5000 1.5% on remainder Half commission on closing	Execution
SHARELINK	Cannon House 24 The Priory Queensway Birmingham B4 6BS 021 200 4585	None	£20 min. £1.50/ contract Scale – 1.5% Half commission on closing	Execution
SHEPPARDS	1 London Bridge London SE1 9QU 071 378 7000	None	£35 min. £1/ contract Scale – 2.5% first £5000 1.5% next £5000 1% on remainder Half commission on closing	Advisory and Execution
TOWNSLEY & CO	44 Worship Street London EC2A 2JT 071 377 6161	£5000	£40 min. £1/ contract Scale – 2% first £5000 1% on remainder	Advisory and Execution

Company	Address/ Tel No	Minimum Account £	Commission & Charges	Services Offered
W H IRELAND STEPHENS & CO	Grange House John Dalton Street Manchester M2 6FW 061 832 6644	None	£30 min. £2/ contract Scale – 2.75% first £5000 2% next £5000 1% on remainder	Advisory
WISE SPEKE	Cutler House 3b Devonshire Square London EC2M 4YA 071 617 2900	None	£30 min. £1.40/contract Scale – 2.5% first £5000 1.5% next £5000 1% on remainder Half commission on closing	Advisory and Execution
WISE SPEKE	Commercial Union House 39 Pilgrim Street Newcastle Upon Tyne NE1 6RQ 091 261 1266	None	£30 min. £1.40/ contract Scale – 2.5% first £5000 1.5% next £5000 1% on remainder Half commission on closing	Advisory and Execution

APPENDIX D

LIFFE index and equity options and their expiry cycles

Jan Apr Jul Oct	**Feb May Aug Nov**
Allied Lyons	BAT Industries
Argyll Group	BTR
Asda	British Aerospace
BAA	British Telecom
Bass	Eastern Electricity
BP	GEC
Beecham	Grand Met
Boots	Guinness
British Airways	Hanson
British Steel	Ladbroke
Cable & Wireless	LASMO
Commercial Union	Lucas Inds
Courtaulds	P & O
Glaxo	Pilkington
HSBC	Prudential
ICI	RTZ
Kingfisher	Redland
Land Securities	Rolls Royce
Marks & Spencer	Royal Ins
Nat West Bank	Tesco
Reuters	Utd Biscuits
Sainsbury J	Vodafone
Shell	Williams Hld
Storehouse	
Thames Water	
Traf House	
Unilever	
Zenaca	

Mar Jun Sep Dec
Abbey National
Amstrad
Barclays

Mar   Jun   Sep   Dec
Blue Circle
British Gas
Dixons
Fisons
Forte
Hillsdown
Lonrho
National Power
Scottish Power
Sears
TSB
Tarmac
Tomkins
Wellcome

Four Closest Months + Jun Dec
FT–SE 100 (American Exercise)

Mar, Jun, Sep, Dec + Two Additional Near Months
FT–SE 100 (European Exercise)

APPENDIX E

Further questions and answers

REVISION QUESTIONS – PART ONE

1 An investor expects a sharp rise in the price of a security. To take advantage of this expected rise he purchases a Nov 140 call at 8. What is the break-even point for the trade at expiry?

A 140
B 148
C 132
D 142

2 An investor sells 10 August 460 puts for a premium of 18. The break-even point at expiry and premium received are

A £1800 and 442
B £1800 and 442
C £1800 and 472
D £18000 and 472

3 The price of ABC Ltd is 289. An investor expects the price to fall slightly over the coming months. Should he

A Buy Puts
B Sell Puts
C Sell Calls
D Buy Calls

4 It is 1 December and an investor expects the price of XYZ Ltd to fall substantially over the next month. The following put options are available:

XYZ Ltd 332

	Feb	May	Aug
300	3	8	12
330	13	22	26
360	42	42	46

Should the investor

    A Buy the Aug 330 put
    B Sell the Feb 360 put
    C Buy the Feb 300 put
    D Sell the May 300 put

5 The index stands at 3289 and an investor holds a 3100 call. The option has an intrinsic value of

    A 3195
    B No intrinsic value
    C 3114
    D 189

6 If an investor exercises a 3100 index call with an EDSP of 3197 he will receive (excluding commission etc.)

    A £970
    B £97
    C £3100
    D £3197

7 Calculate the time value for the following options.

Underlying security 594

	Dec
550	1
600	12
650	58

8 An increase in volatility of an underlying security will result in

    A A decrease in call premiums
    B An increase in put premiums
    C No change in either calls or puts
    D A decrease in put premiums

9 It is 1 June. The European index option will have which of the following expiry dates?

    A Jun, Jul, Aug, Sep, Dec & Mar
    B Jun, Jul, Sep, Dec & Mar
    C Jun, Aug, Sep & Mar
    D Jun, Jul, Aug, Sep & Dec

10 The maximum loss for a writer of a May 160 call option with a premium of 24 is

A 160
B 240
C Unlimited
D 24

REVISION QUESTIONS – PART TWO

1 Buying a call option can be used to
i Gain exposure
ii Maintain exposure
iii Lock in a purchase price
iv Provide downside protection

A i, iii only?
B i, ii only?
C i, ii, iii & iv?
D i, ii, iii only?

2 Selling a call can be used to
i Enhance performance
ii Offset the cost of stock purchase
iii Secure a selling price
iv Provide downside protection

A i, iii only?
B i, ii, iii & iv?
C ii, iii only?
D i, ii only?

3 Buying a put can be used to
i Gain exposure to a price fall
ii Provide insurance
iii Lock in a sale price
iv Lock in a purchase price

A i, ii, iii & iv?
B i, ii only?
C ii, iii only?
D i, ii, iii only?

4 Writing a put can be used to
i Generate additional income
ii Provide downside protection
iii Lock in a purchase price
iv Gain exposure to a price fall

A i, ii only?
B i, iii only?
C ii, iii only?
D iii, iv only?

5 An investor has a portfolio valued at £95,000. With the index standing at 3189 the investor should purchase how many index options to hedge his portfolio?

A 2
B 3
C 4
D 5

6 To deal in traded options a broker must be a member of which of the following organisations?

A LIFFE
B The London Stock Exchange
C The Securities and Investment Board
D The Securities and Futures Authority

7 Which of the following profit and loss profiles are for the following trades?

A Vertical bull spread
B Ratio call spread
C Straddle
D Butterfly

Match the sketch number to the relevent letter.

Sketch 1

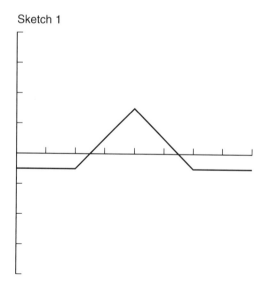

Sketch 2

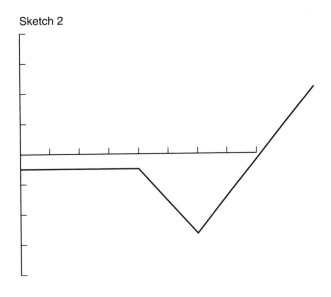

Sketch 3

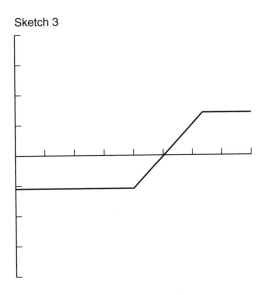

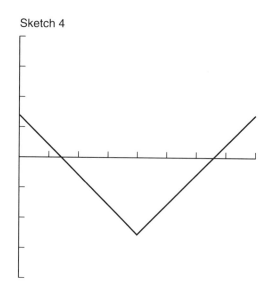

Sketch 4

ANSWERS – PART ONE

1 B

2 A

3 B

4 C

5 D

6 A

7 550 = 1
600 = 6
650 = 2

8 B

9 A

10 C

ANSWERS – PART TWO

1 D

2 B

3 D

4 B

5 B

6 D

7 A = 3
B = 2
C = 4
D = 1

GLOSSARY

Abandon: To allow an option to expire without exercising or trading it.

American option: An option that can be exercised at any time during its life.

Arbitrage: The establishment of risk free profit.

Ask price: The price at which market makers will sell. Also known as the offer price.

Assignment: A notice from the clearing house notifying the writer of an option that he has been exercised against.

At-the-money: An option whose exercise price is the same or almost the same as the underlying security price.

Bar chart: A chart plotting the high, low and closing prices of a security.

Bear spread: A spread designed to make a limited profit from a falling underlying security price.

Bear market: A market in which prices are falling.

Bid price: The price at which market makers will buy an asset.

Binomial pricing model: A pricing model first designed by Cox, Ross and Rubenstein.

Black–Scholes pricing model: An options pricing model designed by Fischer Black and Myron Scholes.

Bonus issue: See Capitalisation issue.

Bottom: A low for a security or a market.

Break-even point: The price at which an option position will neither make nor lose money.

Broker: An individual who transacts business on the options market on behalf of clients.

Bull spread: A spread designed to make a limited profit from a rising underlying security price.

Bull market: A market in which the prices are rising.

Butterfly spread: A combination of a bull and bear spread using three different exercise prices.

Buyer: An investor whose first trade is to purchase an option. Also known as a holder.

Cabinet bid: A bid of 1p for a whole contract which is deep out-of-the-money.

Capitalisation issue: The issue of fully paid new shares to existing share holders.

Clearing house: A company responsible for the registration and settlement of traded options business.

Calendar spread: A spread involving the simultaneous sale of a near dated option with the purchase of a longer dated option. Also known as horizontal or time spread.

Call option: The right, but not the obligation, to buy an asset at an agreed price on or before a given date.

Class: All options of the same type pertaining to the same underlying security. Calls and puts from different classes.

Closing purchase: A transaction in which the writer of an option buys back an option identical to the one sold, thereby extinguishing any obligations.

Closing sale: A transaction in which a buyer sells an option identical to the one held, extinguishing his rights as a holder.

Combination: A spread created by purchasing a call and a put on the same underlying security but with different exercise prices.

Contract: All traded options are bought and sold in contracts. Each contract normally being for 1000 shares. Fractions of contracts cannot be traded.

Covered call write: The writing of call options against a long position in the underlying security.

Covered put write: The writing of a put option against either the short sale of the underlying security or a cash holding sufficient to purchase the stock if exercised against.

Cox, Ross and Rubenstein pricing model: A binomial pricing model designed by Cox, Ross and Rubenstein.

Crowd: A group of market traders for one particular sector.

Cum: A security that comes with all rights and payments.

Delta: A measure of the amount an options fair price will change for a one penny change in the underlying security.

Delta hedge: A hedge in which the amount of contracts purchased is determined by the Delta of the option.

Diagonal spread: A spread in which the exercise price and expiry dates of the options differ.

Dividend: A payment, from the company's post-tax profits, made by a company to its share holders.

Dividend cover: The number of times that a dividend is covered by available profits.

Early exercise: The exercise of an option before its expiry date.

Earnings per share: The amount of profit attributed to share holders divided by the number of shares in issue.

Earnings yield: The earnings per share as a percentage of the current market price.

European option: An option that can only be exercised at expiry.

Exercise: The act, by the holder of an option, to exercise his right and purchase (call) or sell (put) the underlying security.

Exercise notice: A formal notification by a stockbroker to the clearing house that his client wishes to exercise his rights and purchase (call) or sell (put) the underlying security.

Exercise price: The price at which the holder may buy or sell the underlying security. Exercise prices are set by the exchange in accordance with their rules and regulations.

Expiry cycle: The three different cycles for expiry dates.

Expiry date: The last day on which an option may be exercised or traded.

Fair value: The theoretical price of an option derived from a pricing model.

Floor broker: An individual qualified to trade on the options marker floor on behalf of others.

Fungibility: The ability to open and close contracts with different counter parties.

Futures contract: A contract giving the holder the right to buy the underlying security. Unlike an option a holder of a futures contract is obliged to exercise the contract at expiry if the position has not been closed.

Gamma: The amount by which the delta of an option changes for a one penny change in the underlying security.

Gearing: The change in the value of an option when compared to the change in the underlying security.

Hedge: An opposite position in options or the underlying security that increases in value to compensate for a fall in the value of the instrument being hedged.

Historic volatility: The standard deviation of an underlying security obtained from historic prices.

Holder: An investor who opens or increases his position by buying an option.

Implied volatility: The standard deviation of an underlying security obtained from prices currently trading in the market.

Index options: Traded options based on the FT–SE 100 Share Index.

Initial margin: The initial payment made to the clearing house by a writer of an option as part of the margin payment.

In-the-money: A call option whose exercise price is below the current market price of the underlying security or a put option whose exercise price is above the current market price of the underlying security.

Intrinsic value: A call option has intrinsic value when its exercise price is below the current market price of the underlying security; a put option has intrinsic value when its exercise price is above the current market price of the underlying security. Any option that is in-the-money has intrinsic value.

LIFFE: The London International Financial Futures and Options Market.

Line chart: A chart plotting the closing prices of a security connected by a line.

Local: A trader on the market floor who trades for his own account.

Long: The position established by buying (holding) an option.

LTOM: The London Traded Options Market set up by the London Stock Exchange to trade options. LTOM merged with LIFFE in 1992.

Margin: Collateral required from a writer to guarantee he can meet his contractual obligations. A form of insurance in case of being exercised against.

Market maker: A trader who buys and sells securities on behalf of his firm's account.

Mid price: The price of an option or a security midway between the bid and offer price.

Moving averages: A method of smoothing out price fluctuations to obtain a clearer picture of price trends.

Naked call writing: The writing of call options without holding the underlying security.

Naked put writing: The writing of put options without either making a short sale of the underlying security or holding sufficient cash to purchase the stock if exercised against.

Net asset value: The amount by which the assets of a company exceed liabilities.

Normal distribution curve: A method of displaying the probability of different returns on an underlying security or portfolio.

Novation: The process of replacing the counter party of a trade with the clearing house.

Open outcry: The method of trading on LIFFE where all bids and offers are made verbally and are audible to all.

Opening purchase: An initial transaction in which an investor becomes the buyer and holder of an option.

Opening sale: An initial transaction in which an investor writes and sells an option.

Out-of-the-money: A call option whose exercise price is above the current market price or a put option whose exercise price is below the current market price of the underlying security.

Over-the-counter options (OTC): An option, tailored to individual needs, not traded on a recognised exchange.

Pit: An area of trading on a market floor.

Pit observer: A member of the exchange staff responsible for overseeing trading on the market floor.

Portfolio: The combined investments of an investor of fund.

Position: The holding of an investor in a particular security. Either long or short.

Premium: The price of an option, expressed in pence per share, paid by the buyer to the seller.

Price earnings ratio: The ratio of a security's price to the earnings per share.

Price objective: The level to which a security's price is expected to rise or fall.

Pricing model: A mathematical formula designed to generate a fair value of an option.

Public limit order: A firm dealing instruction from a private investor that cannot be executed immediately.

Put–call parity: The relationship between put and call prices that implies the absence of arbitrage opportunities.

Put option: The right,but not the obligation, to sell an asset at an agreed price on or before a given date.

Ratio spread: A spread in which the purchase and sale of options is not equal.

Resistance: A technical analysis term for a price level that the underlying security cannot break. The resistance level is always higher than the current price.

Rights issue: An offer to existing share holders to subscribe to a new issue of shares, usually at a reduced price.

Roll down: The closing of an options position at a high exercise price and the opening of a position with a lower exercise price.

Roll up: The closing of an options position at low exercise price and the opening of a position with a higher exercise price.

SPAN: Standard Portfolio Analysis used in the calculation of margin.

Scrip issue: See Capitalisation issue.

Seller: The writer of an option.

Sell short: To sell a security that an investor does not own.

Series: All options of the same class with the same exercise price and expiry date.

Short: A position established by writing (selling) options.

Spread: An option trade in which a long position is offset by a short position in a different series.

Standard deviation: A measure of the volatility of an underlying security.

Stock Exchange account: A dealing period, normally two weeks, in which all deals completed are settled and paid for on the account day, usually ten days after the end of the account.

Straddle: The simultaneous purchase or sale of the same quantity of calls and puts with the same exercise price and expiry date.

Strike price: The price at which the underlying security can be bought or sold. Also known as the exercise price.

Support level: A technical analysis term for a price level that the underlying security cannot break. The support level is always below the current price.

Synthetic stock: A combination of calls and puts with the same characteristics as the underlying security.

Takeover: One company acquiring the control of a second company by obtaining a majority of voting stock in the target company.

Theta: The change in an option's fair value for a one day reduction in the time to expiration.

Time value: That part of an options premium which reflects the remaining life of an option. Time value is the part of the options premium that exceeds the options intrinsic value. The longer to expiry the greater the time value.

Traditional option: An option that gives the holder the right, but not the obligation, to buy or sell the underlying security. A traditional option may not be traded in any circumstances.

Trend line: A straight line on a chart that connects a series of tops or bottoms forming a trend.

Underlying security: Share on which traded options are based.

Volatility: A measure of the amount of price movement of an underlying security over a given period.

Warrant: A security issued by a company giving the holder the right to subscribe for new stock sometime in the future.

Writer: An investor who transacts an opening sale.

INDEX

American options 31
arbitrage 93
ascending triangle 126
at-the-money 41

binomial pricing tree 176
Black and Scholes pricing 49, 176
bear spread 73
bull spread 71
butterfly spread 78
buyer 10, 19

cab bid 108
calendar spread 73
calls
    buying 19
    writing (selling) 21
capitalisation issue 155
charts 119
Chicago Board Options Exchange 3
Chicago Mercantile Exchange 150
class 12
closing 14
combination 83
contract note 10
contract size 15
covered writing
    call 21
    put 25
Cox, Ross and Rubinstein 49, 178
crowd 107

dealing system 106
delivery 111
delta 180
delta hedge 99, 180
descending triangle 126
diagonal spread 79
dividends 46
dividend cover 131
dividend yield 130
downside protection 63

early exercise 56
earnings per share 129
earnings yield 130
exercise 111
exercise notice 111
exercise price 12
expected returns 173
expiry date 12
European options 31

FIMBRA 169
futures 137
FT–SE 100 31-35

Gamma 181
gearing 49

head and shoulders 125
hedge 34, 68, 96, 139, 180
horizontal spread 77

index options 31-35
interest rates 47
in-the-money 41
intrinsic value 39-41
IMRO 169

Kappa 182
key reversal 124

LAUTRO 169
LIFFE 4, 105
London Clearing House (LCH) 64, 149
London Traded Options Market (LTOM) 3
long 19, 24

margin 23, 64, 149, 156
margin requirements 149
market maker 105-106
moving average 128

naked options writing 59
net asset value 131
non-assented stock 159

normal distribution curve 173-176

offer price 108
opening purchase 15
opening sale 15
open outcry 106
out-of-the-money 41

partial write 103
pension funds 5
pit 107
premium 13
price/earnings ratio 130
price information 16
Public Limit Orders 108
Public Limit Order Board 108
puts
    buying 24
    writing (selling) 25

random selection 174
rectangle 126
regulation 167
Rho 182
rights issue 157
risk 4, 95

Securities and Futures Authority (SFA) 169
series 15
settlement 110

short term trading 128
Securities and Investment Board (SIB) 168
spreads 73-80
Stock Exchange account period 14
stop loss 129
straddle 81
strangle 83
strike price 12
SWAPS 143

takeovers 158
Theta 181
time value 41
trading hours 106
traditional options 141

underlying security 12
unit of trading 14
unit trust 5

Vega 182
vertical spreads 73-75
volatility 45-46, 174-175

walking
    up 54-55
    down 68
wedge 127
writing 21
warrants 140